~

MW00943104

Morning Song

By
David Chaltas

Morning Song
By: David Chaltas

Copyright 2018
All Rights Reserved
Library of Congress Control Number:

ISBN-13: 978-1983818486
ISBN-10: 1983818488

All rights reserved. No part of this book may be reproduced or transmitted in any form or by any means, electronic or mechanical, including photocopying, recording, or by any information storage, and retrieval system, without permission in writing from the copyright owner.

Proudly Printed in the
United States of America

DEDICATION

I must first dedicate this book to our Lord and Savior, Jesus Christ, from whom all blessings flow. I offer a special dedication to three little cherubs that I have never met but think about every day but have nothing but unconditional love for them. May their lives be Christ-filled. To my children and the grandchildren I call Cherubs, I thank you for the time we shared though short. I offer this as a gift of love. May they all find their Morning Song.

"My voice shalt thou hear in the morning, Oh Lord, in the morning I will direct my prayer unto thee and will look up." Psalm 5:3

FOREWORD

Though very personal at times, the author offers insight into difficult times, as well as those most memorable. His stories capture the essence of the trials, troubles, tribulations, and ultimate triumphs that Christians experience. His teachings are Biblically sound and are written to help others on their journey through life.

As Christians, there is no perfect life but rather, there is a way to seek the peace found only in Christ that will sustain you through the trials. Finding freedom through salvation is the beginning of an eternal journey. While on this side of the Jordan, there will be tribulations and weeping, but joy comes in the morning when we cross the turbid veil and all things we be revealed and made new. May you start each day with your morning song…

"Cause me to hear your lovingkindness in the morning, for in you do I trust, cause me to know the way in which I should walk, for I lift up my soul unto you." Psalm 143:8

ABOUT MY BOOK

My book entitled, <u>Morning Song,</u> is a journey. It has taken me from a mourning song to a wondrous Morning Song that lifts me on the wings of love. The selection of prose, poems, and other meanderings is meant to help others realize they are not alone or adrift upon the sea. There is a Rock of Ages that beckons you.

The Bible tells us in Psalm 30:4-5 to *"Sing praises to the Lord, O you his saints, and give thanks to his holy name. for his anger is but for a moment, and his favor is for a lifetime. Weeping may tarry for the night, but joy comes with the morning."*

The lessons of life, for life, compiled within the confines of this book represents reflections upon experiences I have seen or heard. Over the years, my mourning song has turned into a wondrous MORNING SONG where I sing the praises of God for loving me enough to offer His Son in my place on a cross at Calvary.

RECOMMENDED BOOKS BY THE AUTHOR

CHRISTIAN & SELF-HELP LESSONS
Raging Waters
His Amazing Grace
Beneath the Falling Waters
Beyond Peaceful Shores
As Far as the Eye Can See
Beyond the Sunset
Mourning in the Mountains
Beside the Still Waters
In My Father's House
Day Spring
At the Foot of Calvary
In the Shadow of Calvary's Cross

CHILDRENS BOOKS
The Mouse and the Cadillac
A Horse on the Porch
The Little Scrub Pine
Teddy, the Sleepy Bear
Buckwheat
Bo, the Bashful Buffalo
The Jesus Donkey
Blue, the Three-Legged Cat
Sabrina, the Little Ballerina
A Bear in the Basement
The Misadventures of Bubba Lee

TABLE OF CONTENTS

ASSEMBLY OF NOBODIES

I freely admit it. I am a nobody. I go to church
with an assembly of nobodies. They would be the
to concur with my statement.

A friend of mine is a mechanic. He sometimes
comes to church with dirt under his fingernails and
on occasion, poorly clad. All the congregation
welcomes him. He is a nobody that is now a
somebody, because of the Almighty. There is a
businessman who comes in a well-tailored suit.
He is the pillar of the community and gives freely
to the church. He was a nobody until he met the
Almighty, who made him a somebody.

There is a lady that attends the church. She had a
reputation. She was talked about and shunned
until she took off the old cloak of a nobody, put on
the new garment of being a somebody that was
freely given to her by the Almighty. We have this
preacher. For many years he was a nobody. One
day he met the Almighty and became a somebody.
He has served the Great I Am for nearly forty
years.

I was the chief of sinners. I was a back slider,
womanizer, and double tongued in my truths. I did
not deserve salvation. Yet the Almighty took me,
a nobody, and created a somebody. We didn't
deserve His amazing grace. We didn't deserve to

have a peace within us that passes all understanding. We didn't deserve to be somebody. But our Almighty is in the making us all into somebodies.

The Bible, which was inspired by the Almighty, was given to a somebody that used to be a nobody. In His Holy Word, He tells us how to become somebody loved eternally by Him. Listen with your soul His divine words:

Titus 3:5 – *"Not by works of righteousness which we have done, but according to his mercy he saved us, by the washing of regeneration, and renewing of the Holy Ghost."*

John 6:44 – *"No man can come to me, except the Father which hath sent me draw him: and I will raise him up at the last day."*

Ephesians 2:8-9 – *"For by grace are ye saved through faith; and that not of yourselves: [it is] the gift of God."*

Romans 10:9 – *"That if thou shalt confess with thy mouth the Lord Jesus, and shalt believe in thine heart that God hath raised him from the dead, thou shalt be saved."*

Ephesians 2:8 – *"For by grace are ye saved*

through faith; and that not of yourselves: [it is] the gift of God."

John 14:6 – *"Jesus saith unto him, I am the way, the truth, and the life: no man cometh unto the Father, but by me."*

Acts 4:12 – *"Neither is there salvation in any other: for there is none other name under heaven given among men, whereby we must be saved."*

Friend, are you tired of being a nobody? Are you sick and tired of being sick and tired? Are you ready to be transformed into a somebody? The Almighty calls you. The Almighty beckons you? The Almighty longs for you to come home.

This is a good time to find your 'morning song' and change your life forever. It's not complicated at all. For God gave His son because He loved you and wanted you to have everlasting life. He wants you to be His own. Friend today is the day of salvation and you can be a saved somebody and find your morning song of praise.

SET ME FREE

I had occasion to attend a wondrous church in Okeechobee, Florida. As I walked up to the door, a man by the name of Tom greeted me, and welcomed me to the First Baptist Church. I thanked him and asked him where to enter. He pointed to the lower door and to the stairway that led the balcony. I chose the stairs.

I went in quietly and sat in the balcony overlooking the pulpit as a praise and worship song was being sung. I noted the congregation was intently and contently listening, as well as mouthing the words. The music was soothing and set the mood for the preacher.

A young man stepped forward and I could not help but note his youthful appearance. But once he began offering the sermon, I realized that indeed he was the minister. His passion for the gospel was evident and his message was riveting.

He talked of Galatians 5: 1-26, and titled the sermon, 'Set me free'. As he read the passage, I realized how important it was for me to be free in the spirit and not be tied to secular things. The Bible teaches us in verse one to, *"Stand fast therefore in the liberty wherewith Christ hath made us free and be not entangled again with the yoke of bondage."* Sometimes we get so caught up in this secular structure that we forget we have a higher calling to abide by God's rules.

We abide by the rules of society, even to the point of letting them overshadow God's laws. We forget that our first duty is to Him. We have examples in the Bible. Daniel, who was thrown into the lion's den because of his belief. Shadrack, Meshack, and Abednego respectfully disobeyed the law of their earthly king (Nebuchadnezzar) in order to follow their heavenly king. They didn't bow, they didn't bend, and they didn't abandon their beliefs. They took negative situations; even life-threatening experiences and showed others how to obey the laws of God.

Jesus taught us to *"Render to Caesar the things that are Caesar's, and to God the things that are God's."* (Mark 12:17) But he also showed us to stand tall against wrongdoing (example: turning over the tables in the temple, calling out the high priests for their hypocrisy) and to resist the devil's temptations.

As I listened to the message, a sudden chill came over me. I felt a mysterious presence, a peace within me and I sensed that I was to do something. From out of nowhere, a title to another book came. It was simply, Morning Song. I realized that I my spirit was telling me that I must begin a new book devoted to sharing my morning song (that began as my 'mourning song') to help others realize theirs.

It was my beginning. It started in a church and was meant to be shared with others. But my morning song doesn't preach to the choir. Rather, it reaches out to those who also have or are struggling. It is a book designed to show that with Christ, we are more than conquerors. We can take the negatives of life (and they will continue to come) and change them to a song of rejoicing. That is my daily mission in the morning.

As I left the church, I was filled with a renewal, spirit was uplifted, and my morning song was that of praise.

MY MOURNING SONG

There was an old show called 'He Haw' way back when. I can recall a particular song that used to sum up my attitude about life. It went, *"Gloom, despair, agony on me. Deep, dark depression, excessive misery. If it weren't for bad luck, I'd have no luck at all. Gloom despair, and agony on me."* For years, the song depicted my view of the world. I guess I was on the pity potty.

I found myself mourning for what might have been. I mourned for my father that was taken from me one day after my sixth birthday. I mourned for not knowing him and having that male model I so desperately needed in my life. I mourned for a man to say that he loved me and that I was important to him. I mourned.

I mourned for the friends I left behind when we moved. I mourned for those childhood possessions left behind that meant so much to me. I mourned for my dog and worried about him every day. I longed to go back to my Pine Haven.

I mourned for my beloved children as I realized I could not be the father I wanted to be. I mourned because of the broken relationship that existed between my ex-lady. I bemoaned and felt the pangs of longing every day for the sound and sight of my little ones.

I mourned for what I had lost in terms of my strong childhood faith that was taken from me by those who ridiculed me. I mourned for my mother who endured such in order to have what she thought was love. I mourned for the child within and wished I could relive those precious moments of innocence.

Then came the realization. I mourned not knowing that the trials of life were exactly what I needed in order to mold and shape me into what I was my destiny. I came to the point of recognizing that my choices determined my mourning song. It took surrendering all to Him for me to change my mourning song into my morning song!

Now, I still have the problems of life facing my daily. But I have something that can't be taken from me. I have a morning song. It is not of gloom and despair but one of being a beautiful day! I find myself eager to see what grand adventures await me and I know that God will be beside me.

If I stumble, He's there. If I falter, He's there. If I fail, He's there. He stands by me. He will never forsake me. He told me that He will never forsake me or leave me as an orphan. He will come to me! He has given me a morning song!

I have determined that the first fifteen minutes of me day creates my mind set and establishes my mood. So, I wake up to the sound of music in my heart. I offer a prayer. I do my morning devotions. But most of all, I sing my morning song.

What is my song, you ask? There are so many. Most of the time it is the music of my soul rejoicing. Sometimes it is the peace filled words of In the Garden. Listen to the first stanza: *"I come to the garden alone, while the dew is still on the roses, and the voice I hear falling on my ear, the Son of God discloses. And He walks with me, and He talks with me, and He tells me I am His own. And the joy we share as we tarry there, none other has ever known."*

There are so many more like *"Blessed Assurance, Jesus is mine! Oh, what a foretaste of glory divine! Heir of salvation, purchase of God, Born of His spirit, washed in His blood."* And of course, *"Amazing Grace, how sweet the sound that saved a wretch like me. I once was lost but no I'm found. Was blind but now I see."*

Friend, I pray this day, no matter your troubles or sorrows, you find YOUR Morning Song and let it last you forever and a day.

BE ENCOURAGED

As I got ready for church, I noted that autumn was upon me. The leaves were beginning to change, a mist clung to the ground, the air seemed to be heavier than usual, and the smell of fall was in the air. I had gotten used to summer that I had not noticed it was fading into the fall season.

As I walked through the doors of the Letcher Baptist Church, I wondered what the topic of the sermon would be. I was once again amazed at how God knows our needs and offers us opportunities to reflect upon them if we will only our hearts. Preacher Jones announced the sermon and it hit me like a ton of bricks: Be encouraged.

He shared from the Old Testament. the book of Joshua 1:1-18. He noted 4 verses in which God heartened unto Joshua to not get discouraged and to rely upon Him. He says to Joshua to, *"Be strong and of a good courage"*. (Verses 6, 7, 9, 18) God tells Joshua that, *"I will not fail thee, nor forsake thee."* Verse 9 offers us such hope: "Do not be afraid; do not be discouraged, for the Lord your God will be with you wherever you go."

He went on and talked about the Hebrews that fled Egypt and how Moses lifted up his rod and God parted the Red Sea. As they crossed, the scriptures say that the bottom of the sea was dry! A cloud led them and Manna from heaven was given unto them each day. They witnessed miracles! Yet they became apathetic and grew tired of the same routine. They became dispirited, turned from God, and wanted something new. Their indifference, lethargic thinking led them away from God Almighty to the point they made golden idols to worship.

Being a preacher of over forty years, he mentioned that he probably preached over 200 sermons a year and in some cases, he preached closed to 300. How easy it would be to become 'callused', burnt out, and/or overly accustomed to the routine. The secret to fighting such weapons of the deceiver is to pray, seek His guidance, study God's word, and meditate upon the sacred principles of the gospel. Be led by faith of things to come and things to hope for.

The Bible tells us in James 4:8, to, *"Draw nigh to God, and he will draw nigh to you. Cleanse your hands, ye sinners; and purify your hearts, ye double minded."*

Friend, God is with you always. He will not abandon you. He is your source of renewal. *"But those who hope in the Lord will renew their strength. They will soar on wings like eagles; they will run and not grow weary, they will walk and not be faint."* (Isaiah 40:31)

my favourite verse

He is our helper, our healer, our redeemer. In Psalm 121:1-2, David captures his source of strength: *"I lift up my eyes to the mountains— where does my help come from? My help comes from the Lord, the Maker of heaven and earth."*

Again, the preacher reminded me in his sermon to be bold and to, *"Be on your guard; stand firm in the faith; be courageous; be strong"* I Corinthians 16:13

For Devotion

Friends Sometimes in life we all need to be renewed. We are creatures of habit and tend to get bored with the everyday things of life. We become complacent, take things for granted and bored. Then we began looking for something new. That is the deceiver's way of manipulating you. The grass is not greener on the other side. He does it at work, he does it at home and he does it in the church. We must put on the breastplate God has provided and be constantly aware of the stalker's desire to destroy you.

That is why we must be courageous and strong, trusting in His words that, *"I will not abandon you, I will not leave you as orphans, I will come to you."* John 14:18

"When you pass through the waters, I will be with you; and when you pass through the rivers, they will not sweep over you. When you walk through

the fire, you will not be burned; the flames will not set you ablaze." Isaiah 43:2

Friends, this day, and every day, let your morning song be that of praise, renewal, and faith. Let love dominate your heart and joy permeate your soul. Let your morning song be so obvious that others will hear it and say, *"If that is religion, if that is salvation, if that joy in the morning, I MUST HAVE IT."*

I BELIEVE

"Be anxious for nothing, but in everything by prayer and supplication with thanksgiving let your requests be made known to God. And the peace of God, which surpasses all comprehension, will guard your hearts and your minds in Christ Jesus.
Philippians 4:6-7

I believe in the basic goodness of people. I believe in happiness. I believe in joy. I believe in peace. I believe in love. I believe in peace through Christ. I also believe all my desires, all my needs will be met, according to His glory. I am truly blessed.

There are those who do not understand. They dwell in darkness. They have either not found the light or have rejected it. They do not know how to be surrender all.

There is a wondrous poem written by Max Ehrmann. Max was born in 1972 and died in 1945. He studied at DePaul and later at Harvard. He was a lawyer and author. He is best known for his poem Desiderata (Latin word for 'Things Desired').

His poem has been shared with millions upon millions and contains within the perimeter of the words, truths. His writings often were on spiritual subjects. Listen to his words with your heart.

Desiderata
By Max Ehrmann

Go placidly amid the noise and haste and
remember what peace there may be in silence.
As far as possible, without surrender, be on good
terms with all persons.
Speak your truth quietly and clearly; and listen to
others,
even to the dull and ignorant; they too have their
story.
Avoid loud and aggressive persons, they are
vexations to the spirit.
If you compare yourself with others, you may
become vain and bitter,
for always there will be greater and lesser persons
than yourself.
Enjoy your achievements as well as your plans.
Keep interested in your own career, however
humble;
it is a real possession in the changing fortunes of
time.
Exercise caution in your business affairs, for the
world is full of trickery.
But let this not blind you to what virtue there is;
many persons strive for high ideals,
and everywhere life is full of heroism.
Be yourself. Especially do not feign affection.
Neither be cynical about love;
for in the face of all aridity and disenchantment it

is as perennial as the grass.
Take kindly the counsel of the years, gracefully
surrendering the things of youth.
Nurture strength of spirit to shield you in sudden
misfortune.
But do not distress yourself with dark imaginings.
Many fears are born of fatigue and loneliness.
Beyond a wholesome discipline, be gentle with
yourself.
You are a child of the universe no less than the
trees and the stars;
you have a right to be here. And whether or not it
is clear to you,
no doubt the universe is unfolding as it should.
Therefore, be at peace with God, whatever you
conceive Him to be.
And whatever your labors and aspirations, in the
noisy confusion of life,
keep peace with your soul. With all its sham,
drudgery, and broken dreams,
it is still a beautiful world. Be cheerful. Strive to be
happy.

I believe that the items and all things desired can
be found through Christ. He is your peace. He is
your joy. He is your salvation. He is your serenity.
He mends hurting hearts. This I believe. He is
your morning song.

I SURRENDER ALL

"And we know that in all things God works for the good of those who love him, who have been called according to his purpose." Romans 8:28

As I entered the little church at the mouth of Spring Branch, I heard a distinct voice within saying, "Be still and know that I am God" (Psalm 46:10). This Sunday I felt depleted. The well had run dry and I needed renewal. The Cherokee have a saying. It goes, *"Listen! Or your tongue will make you deaf."* This was the cause of my spirit's depletion. I had offered lessons of life, for life to others, but had not embraced renewal when opportunity knocked. This sermon was for me to be replenished. I would not be disappointed.

Parson Jones began with the verse that speaks to us all. He shared Romans 8:28 and reassured the congregation that in all things God works for the good of those who love him. That includes the good, the bad, and the ugly. We cannot see around the bend or curve, but our God can because He created them!

He gave the analogy of a piece of iron. When you throw it in the water, what happens? It sinks. But when you take pieces of metal, weld them into a shape and create a boat, it floats. Each individual piece would fail to thrive and sink to the bottom of the water but when welded together, each piece, each experience, each bolt creates something that will carry one across the seas no matter how turbulent they become.

For some reason, that gave me such a sense of comfort and piece. Each experience in our lives have purpose and it is not our time to know. One day will come when all things will be revealed, and we will realize why bad things happen to good people and why God allows choices.

He is always there for us. One day we will understand. While upon this earth we must surrender all and trust in Him. After all, that is what faith is all about.

After the sermon, he closed with an invitation, as the congregation sang, I surrender all. After the sermon, I felt a renewal. I realized that I had not been surrendering all and that I had not taken God at His word. Something led me to research the invitational hymn that moved me to tears of joy.

I surrender all was written by Judson W. Van DeVenter. He was born in 1865 and became an art teacher and musician. He later became a minister and in 1896, he wrote the words to the hymn.

When asked about his song, he shared the following: *"For some time, I had struggled between developing my talents in the field of art and going into full-time evangelistic work. At last the pivotal hour of my life came, and I surrendered all. A new day was ushered into my life. I became an evangelist and discovered down deep in my soul a talent hitherto unknown to me. God had hidden a song in my heart, and touching a tender chord, He caused me to sing."*

Van DeVenter traveled extensively and in his lifetime, wrote over sixty hymns. Upon his death, the words, 'I surrender all' were inscribed upon his tombstone.

I SURRENDER ALL

All to Jesus I surrender,
All to Him I freely give;
I will ever love and trust Him,
In His presence daily live.

Refrain:
I surrender all,
I surrender all;
All to Thee, my blessed Savior,
I surrender all.

All to Jesus I surrender,
Humbly at His feet I bow;
Worldly pleasures all forsaken,
Take me, Jesus, take me now.

All to Jesus I surrender,
Make me, Savior, wholly Thine;
Let me feel the Holy Spirit,
Truly know that Thou art mine.

All to Jesus I surrender,
Lord, I give myself to Thee;
Fill me with Thy love and power,
Let Thy blessing fall on me.

All to Jesus I surrender,
Now I feel the sacred flame;
Oh, the joy of full salvation!
Glory, glory, to His Name!

"So likewise, whosoever he be of you that forsaketh not all that he hath, he cannot be my disciple." Luke 14:33

"Then answered Peter and said unto him, Behold, we have forsaken all, and followed thee; what shall we have therefore?" Matthew 19:27

THE LAST NATIVITY SCENE

I was caught off guard and didn't see it coming. She left without warning on Christmas eve. I wore my grief like a red badge of despair. I was devastated.

I hadn't celebrated Christmas for several years. Christmas had lost its meaning. The joy and spirit had left me. In fact, I still had all those gifts so gingerly and lovingly wrapped, hidden in the closet. I was likened unto Scrooge. I threw away the tree, some of the ornaments that adorned the tree, and vowed there would never be another tree or Nativity scene displayed in my house. After all, I blamed God for taking her from me.

I don't know how it happened, but I began distancing and isolating myself from others. Whenever someone knocked, I would not answer the door. If they did make it into the house, the conversation was strained and uncomfortable. Even my children became estranged from me because of my gloom and foolish pride. Soon, I got my wish of being left alone.

For the longest time, I was alone in a house that loved built and a house now filled with cobwebs of resentment and pity. I, in fact, had become the most bitter of men. I had become a recluse and miser of misery. The smell of resentment permeated the walls and loneliness became my only friend. I lived that way for years.

My awakening came after Thanksgiving and as the dreaded Christmas season was upon me. I had just returned to the house and was putting up groceries. After I had restocked for my self-imposed siege, I emptied my pockets and placed the change on the table by the forgotten closet. As I turned, I accidently knocked the table over, and my money splattered everywhere. I picked up what I could find lying on the floor but knew that some of the money had inadvertently rolled under the closet door. Reluctantly, I opened the door. With the help of a flashlight, I managed to gather a few coins but saw something shiny. Fearing it was a valued coin, I decided to investigate.

The closet was full of unopened presents, and I was in no mood to bother with them. I hastily dug through them to the shiny object that had caught my eye. As I stepped closer to my goal, I heard something crunch underneath my feet. I immediately stepped back and there it was. The tiny manger that had meant so much to her. It was shattered in pieces.

For some unknown reason, I began to cry and shake with such emotion that my grief could not be contained. I had destroyed the little manger she valued more than anything. The Nativity scene had been her grandmothers, and each piece was priceless to her. The manger had been damaged years ago, but she had painstakingly rebuilt it. Now the manger appeared to be destroyed beyond repair!

Through my anguish I suddenly realized that the baby figure was not in the manger. Through clouded eyes I franticly, but carefully, began moving gifts from Christmas past out of the closet. Then the shiny object caught my eye. There, next to a coin I had desperately searched for, was the Baby Jesus.

My first thought was how did it get separated from the rest of the Nativity scene. Was this a sign? I felt so guilt ridden and burdened. I picked up the little baby and fell to my knees. For the first time in a long time I prayed. The prayer was one of anguish, passion, and brokenness. Oh God, how could I have slipped so far? I sought forgiveness, and for the longest time I did not move from the kneeling position; for I had nowhere else to go.

Then something that I will never be able to explain happened. I felt a presence that I had thought I had lost. In truth, the presence I felt within my being hadn't forsaken me, but rather I had forsaken him. I felt a new burst of freedom and a redemption that I did not deserve. I felt alive again.

I decided that I would unwrap the gifts from a time long ago. As I did so, I smiled at the love that once danced within my heart. Oh, how precious were the memories that I had ran from and abandoned. For some reason, I didn't feel regret, I didn't feel resentment, and I didn't feel anger. I just felt forgiveness, along with love.

As I finished opening most of the gifts, a small box wrapped in a shiny red paper with a green ribbon caught my eye. I decided to open it. It was another gift from her. After I unwrapped the gift, I pulled out a coffee cup from the box. On the mug was engraved words of enlightenment for my soul. The words were, "Treasure the times we have".

Again, the tears fell like morning dew on the meadows. But this time the tears were not of remorse or regret. They were tears of gratitude and self-forgiveness. They were tears of love for a time long forgotten or hidden by the pride within a soiled soul.

I don't know how long I sat among the gifts, and wrinkled, torn, wrapping paper while holding the cup. It really didn't matter though because I was dealing with what I called the 'reckoning'. How wrong I had been! I hadn't treasured those memories. Instead, I had forgotten the meaning of those precious memories and times we had, I replaced them with the sorrow of what might have been. As I sat there, I realized it was time to let go and let God. It was time to rebuild my life before it passed me by. But how?

Then I remembered the manger. I rushed to my feet and picked up every piece of it I could find. I carefully placed them in a jewelry box that belonged to her. I then went to a store and purchased a beautiful tree, lights, and decoration for it, along with outside décor befitting the season. I smiled, laughed, and cried joyfully as I paid for the ornaments. I am sure the clerk wondered about my mental state.

As I loaded down my truck, I realized I had forgotten to look for a manger to replace the one I had broken. I returned to the store and looked everywhere for a Nativity scene befitting the occasion. To my dismay, they were sold out. I went home and once I unloaded my purchases, I decided to continue my quest for a manger worthy of the one she so loved. Time was running out.

As I looked for the Nativity scene in store after store, I began to realize that all the lights and ornaments didn't mean anything without the manger and the Christ Child. When I asked about the Nativity scene, some stores even stated they didn't carry them anymore. I asked why, and I was informed that it wasn't a hot selling item. How could that be, I wondered. Was not Christmas about the birth of Christ and the manner in which the Wise Men, Shepherds, and even the animals paid homage to the King of Kings? Had I been so blind for so long that I didn't see such a changing world? Then I felt the pang of guilt knowing that I too had forgotten the true meaning of Christmas for such a long time. Once again, my heart pleaded for forgiveness.

It was almost closing time when I entered the last store. I desperately looked around for that magical manger but without success. There were presents galore still on the shelves. Everyone dashed around looking for that last minute gift as I looked for the manger: the true meaning of Christmas. The shoppers seemed so preoccupied with shopping that they ignored others, argued over who was in line first, and even raised their voices in anger at one another.

For some reason I yelled out Merry Christmas! The response was silence, and I was given a look like a deer in the headlights. I didn't care, for my heart was filled with Christmas cheer, and besides, I was on a manger mission.

I continued my quest, but it proved to be fruitless. I was distraught as I walked towards the door. For some reason I glazed at the lowest shelf and to my relief, there was the last Nativity scene display. Eureka! Now my set would be complete once again, and I could celebrate the season with the festivities I had lost years ago.

As I picked up the pieces of the Nativity scene and put them in the box, a little boy walked by with his mother and saw the remaining pieces of the display that I had not packed. One of the pieces was the manger containing Baby Jesus. His eyes lit up with wonder, and he tugged on his mother's coat.

"Momma look over there! Baby Jesus is in a manger and he don't have a home! Can we take him home with us?"

The mother shook her head and gently said no. But the little boy was determined in his efforts.

"Mommy, you can have all the money in my piggy bank. Baby Jesus needs a home. We have room. Can't we take him with us? Please! He could take the place of my baby brother that went to be with my daddy in heaven."

Again, the mother shook her head and simply said, *"Son we don't have the money to buy the scene. We don't have enough money for gifts, and besides that nice old man is going to buy Baby Jesus and give him a home."*

Tears streamed down the young mother's face as she slowly walked away. I found myself overcome with emotions that had been restrained for so many years. For all these years I was fully able to celebrate the birth of this baby Jesus, but I had not. Yet this little boy was willing to give everything he had just to give baby Jesus a home. I knew what I had to do.

"Excuse me miss, I could not help but overhear what you son said. I really don't need this Nativity scene, and he looks like he would take care of baby Jesus for me. It is my Christmas gift to you and your precious child," I stated while holding back the tears and sobs.

"Sir, I couldn't accept that. It is too much money," she answered.

"Young lady, you don't know what joy it would give this old man if you would take baby Jesus and give him a home. Besides, I have a nice Nativity scene waiting on me at my home."

She smiled a smile of gratitude and I continued packing the items. The last one to be placed in the box was the manger. Without her seeing me do it, I took out my wallet and placed all the money I had, which amounted to over four hundred dollars, beneath the Christ child and the manger. Then I closed the lid. My heart smiled with the thought of the discovery when they opened the Nativity scene.

I carried the little boy's treasure to the cashier and paid for it with my credit card. I carried the box out to the young lady's old beat up car and delicately placed the cargo into her truck. The little boy was so excited.

"Thank you so much sir, you have made our Christmas," the young mother said with gratefulness in your eyes.

"No madam, you are mistaken. You have made mine," I said with a trembling voice that I had not heard or felt in years.

She gave me a hug, then the little boy ran up to me and wrapped his arms around my leg. So, this Christmas, I thought to myself. It's not too late. I can still celebrate with my loved ones that I had driven off so long ago. But first things first.

I rushed home empty-handed but filled with a renewal of love in my heart. I went straight to the Nativity scene and placed the pieces under the tree. I found the jewelry box containing shattered pieces of the manger. I took them to the kitchen table, and there I worked for hours gluing and mending the broken manger. As I worked I realized that I was not only fixing the fragmented manger, but also, I was mending my broken heart. The manger and I became one.

I finished my project in the early morning hours of Christmas day. After it had thoroughly dried, I took the manger, gently picked up the Christ Child, and placed him in the manger. I plugged in the tree, adjusted the star on top, shined the light on the manger scene, and stepped back. For some reason I spontaneously broke out in song. *Away in the manger, no crib for a bed, the little Lord Jesus lay down his sweet head. The stars in the sky*

*looked down where he lay. The little Lord Jesus
asleep on the hay.*

I also recalled those beautiful words to Silent
Night, and once again tears of gratitude steamed
unabated down my face. I knew what I had to do.
I gathered myself up, left my foolish pride at
home, climbed into my car, and drove towards a
house that I had not visited for several years. I
pulled up in the driveway and sat for a few minutes
praying. I got out of my car, walked up to the
door, and knocked...

That year, I had found the greatest gift of all and
shared it with my children and grandchildren. It
was the gift of forgiveness. It was the gift of love,
made possible by a little boy needing to take our
Lord Jesus home with him. It was the greatest gift
I had ever received, and it was all because of a
child, a manger, and the last Nativity scene.

THE LAST NATIVITY

I searched for the manger
But it could not be found.
It was a complete stranger
To those shopping around.

I looked in the windows
But all I could see

Presents, cell phones, and Kindles
Under the Christmas tree.

The hustle and the bustle
Of frantic shoppers' splurge.
The rustle and the tussle
Of stepping on others' nerves.

I sought to find the Christ child
In the department stores.
The salesclerk said with a smile
The manger is no more.

But wait, there in the corner!
Where eyes could barely see.
Hidden by the adorners:
The last Nativity.

I rushed to its rescue
From the bottom shelf.
But there in plain view
Was a pint-sized little elf.

He whispered to his mother
'Can we take the baby home?
I could be his brother.
He has no place of his own.'

The mother hesitated,
As tears merged in her eyes.

'We don't have the money, we have to wait.'
Then she began to cry.

Overcome with an emotion,
I actually thought I lost,
I gave her my devotion
Well above what the scene cost.

She thanked me for my kindness.
For my generosity.
They took away my blindness
With the last Nativity.

I wished them Merry Christmas:
Not Happy Holidays.
During that short-lived isthmus,
I found the manger's bouquet.

I went home empty handed,
Yet filled with Christmas cheer.
I did what He commanded
And will do so throughout the year.
(Taken from I AM WHITE FROG, by D. Chaltas)

THE CHRISTMAS BLESSING

As I drove towards Stuart, Florida, on a lovely afternoon just two days before Christmas, my mind wandered to my grandchildren. Yet, another year without seeing them. As the years had gone by without one glance at my cherubs faces, it had taken a toll on me. Would they know who I was? Would they be told about me? So many unwanted questioned flooded my mind.

I stopped at my usual haunts looking and thinking how cute that would be for the girls. Then realization once again haunted me. Maybe next year, I thought to myself. It was a fleeting thought in a futile attempt to reassure myself.

I enjoyed shopping at the Nautical but Nice shop and hitting the huge flea market. There was solace as I looked and thought how excited the little ones would be when they saw all of the seashells and other objects from the ocean. Then I thought of how their eyes would show fear at the huge stuffed alligators that were on exhibit. Maybe they would tightly clutch my hand as we walked passed them. My imaginings continued.

I hadn't eaten anything, nor had I visited the beach. I thought I would kill two birds with one stone and grab a hotdog at the Chef Shack next the sand dunes at Stuart beach. I drove to A1A and crossed the bridges saddling St. Lucie River and Indian River Lagoon. I parked and walked amongst families simply enjoying the warmth of the sun and the sea breeze. A sense of loss permeated my being as I coveted what they possessed. I found myself beginning to be filled with self-loathing and despair. Why did I come to this place, I thought to myself?

I ordered my food and sat at the table eating. Across from me was a mother with three girls. I speculated that they ranged in age from nine to thirteen. My mind wandered to another place and for just a moment, I saw those grandbabies in the unknown family. When reality awakened me, my mood was darkened.

I lost my appetite. I threw away a half-eaten hot dog and chips and walked on the planks to the pagodas. As I watched, I noted that two pine trees had been brought and placed in the sand. Several young people were decorating them. I laughed to myself when I realized they were putting seashells, star fish and driftwood as ornaments. They were enjoying decorating and the season. My mood lightened somewhat.

After gazing into the ocean and feeling the breeze carry her kiss to my cheek, I decided to walk along the shoreline. The beach was fairly crowded, and I noted the spirit of the people seemed to be in a Christmas mood.

Then came the young boy playing rap with the volume of his device turned wide open. He walked right by the young people surrounding the Christmas trees and not once offered to turn his device down. I wanted to chastise him. Yielding to better judgement, I decided against such actions. I decided to leave. My mood darkened once again. So, this is Christmas, I thought.

I made it to the boardwalk and as I walked up the planks, I noted an elderly gentleman sitting on one of the benches. What caught my attention was his demeanor and his smile? He was wearing a Hawaiian type shirt decorated with Santa scenes. He had knee high leggings that I summated were to assist with the circulation in his feet and legs. He was rounded in stature and sported a white beard. In fact, I thought he could pass for Santa. As I got closer, I heard him telling people walking by, *"Merry Christmas"*. That was the first time I ever heard someone on a beach wishing such a blessing to strangers.

As I passed him, I looked away to avoid his gaze but was captured by his greeting.

"Merry Christmas, young man," He said.

Without looking, I knew he was addressing me, although he was mistaken about my age.

"Merry Christmas to you," I said halfheartedly.

"What a lovely day to be alive," He stated.

"Yes, I guess it is," I said in the voice of Eeyore.

"Do you live around here, son?" He inquired.

"No, I'm just visiting," I replied.

"Home is where your heart is, and no matter where you are, this life live well," he stated.

For a moment that startled me because that saying is one of my catch phrases. I use it on several of my correspondences. Now this old centurion had my full attention.

"I love coming to the beach. You can smell the fresh breath of God flowing on the wind. Never did like the cold that much, but a man had to make a living. Plus, God created it, so it must be for the good of mankind," He chuckled.

That laugh seemed so familiar, but I couldn't put a finger on it.

"You know son, I'm a very old man. I've been on this earth for many years. I have socks older than you," He said with a burst of laughter.

"One thing I have learned in my years is that a person is as happy as he chooses to be. Take me for example. I haven't talked to my children in several years and wouldn't know my grandkids if they walked through my door. But this I know. They are loved by me and no matter what, my DNA flows in their blood and someday they will remember who I was and that I made them who they are. That is the way of life. Roots and wings is what I gave them, along with unconditional love."

He fell silent for a couple of minutes. I think he was giving me time to soak in his words. Again, he was saying what I had thought. How did he know?

He continued. *"God in His heaven has a plan for us all. He gives us free will to choose. Sometimes we forget that our children have that same will. God doesn't love us any less because of our choices, He simply wants us to repent and come home. You know, like the prodigal. You know how that turned out don't you,"* He stated in a matter of fact manner.

I found myself getting uncomfortable. His words were hitting home like he knew my inner thoughts.

"Don't worry Dave, it'll be alright. Just trust in him and someday your heart's desire will be granted. He'll keep sending you angels," He said as he glanced towards the ocean.

"It's a lovely day, my boy. Have yourself a Merry Christmas." He stated.

This was the opening I wanted. I reciprocated a Christmas greeting and quickly walked away. The closer I got to my car, the more his words sunk into my being. How perceptive he was. Then it hit me like a ton of bricks! He called me Dave! How did he know my name? And wait: He said something that didn't catch until that very moment. He said, "He'll keep sending you angels," My God! My favorite song is, He Keeps Sending Me Angels! How did he know?

I decided to go back and since he lightened my burden, I went to my truck and found one of the books I had written. I would give him a gift for Christmas for being such an insightful and delightful old man. In reality, I wanted to give him something because he gave something priceless to me: a sense of comfort and hope.

I went back to the gazebo, but he had already left. There was a very elderly lady sitting on the same bench that the aged sage had been sitting. Funny, I hadn't noticed her before. I smiled at her and asked her if she saw the gentleman in question.

I described him to her and she paused for a moment before speaking. She asked me to describe him again. I did so. I noticed a strange look came over her.

"Young man, I can assure you that no one has been on this bench for the past hour. This was my husband's favorite spot. This is where we came to when we were much younger. This is where we would sit and watch our children play in the sand. This is the bench where he told stories and shared about loving life and embracing the 'what ifs' as if they were true. This is the sand that held my husband's feet when he walked upon this earth." She stopped to regain her composure.

"Every Christmas he would come and sit on this bench and wish those passing by a Merry Christmas. It was his passion to cheer up others and to make them feel God's goodness no matter their circumstance. He was a man beyond his time and his words touched so many. He was a very wise man of God."

I thanked her and asked if it would be possible for me to give him my book as a gift. Her eyes softened, as she reached out her hand to me.

"Young man, there is no doubt you talked to my husband, or rather HE talked to you. I will take your gift to him and read it to him every day. There is no doubt he will listen with his soul. Son, my dear husband passed away three days ago."

I was stunned. Could it be true? Did I talk to an angel unaware? As I reached out my hand, she patted it, and gently took my book. My silence was deafening! I was without words, but I saw in her eyes gratitude and truth that set me free from all my anxieties. I saw within her countenance a peace and I left with a realization that she would soon join her beloved husband. I had been blessed by the encounter of both. One was on one side of the Jordan, the other waiting across on the peaceful shore.

That man, whose name I will never know, touched me, and knew my pain. He took my thoughts, my anguish, and my bitterness towards himself and was like a sounding board for my reflection. He was more than Santa. He was a man among angels. He was there near the beach where I received my Christmas blessing...

OUR FATHER

I recall the very first time I heard these words. It was in school! Amazed? You shouldn't be my friend. Because in those days, values were taught, along with manners. Bible verses were read, prayers were said, and we honored our Christian nation. In fact, I learned to recite the sacred words below while in a little one room school in Red Oak, Michigan. We weren't asked, but rather told what to study and that included learning Bible verses. After learning a certain number of verses and reciting them to our teacher, we were given the prize of going to a vacation Bible School without paying one cent. We all prayed for the chance of going to a summer camp. We prayed but where did those sacred words come from?

Over two thousand years ago, he gave us the supplication to His Father. He offered it his followers and to any that would listen. He gave it on a hillside by the Sea of Galilee. It is the oldest Christian prayer given unto us and it changed the way we pray.

Looking at the first two words of the petition to our Heavenly Father, Jesus's unselfishness nature amazes me. There he was, the Son of God, and yet offers us His Father as our own. Think of a Father's love for his child. Jesus talked directly to *'Our Father'* and knew where he resided. *'Which art in heaven'* are words showing us His Father's home and where Christ would return.

Then Jesus teaches us to praise God: *'Hallowed be thy name'*. The word 'Hallowed' means holy, revered, consecrated, and sacred. Here our Christ is proclaiming the glory of His/Our Father.

'Thy kingdom come' refers to the second coming of Christ and the gathering of the saints. It is a request that His kingdom be fully established. It is but one of Christ's statements about God's domain.

'Thy will be done on earth as it is in heaven' are words asking God to use us to fulfill His wishes. One of the hardest things we do as humans is to accept God's will. Yet, He loved us so much that he gave us a will of our own, so we could choose to abide by His laws and will. Isn't He an amazing and awesome God?

Whenever I say, *'Give us this day our daily bread'* I realize that Jesus is telling us that His/Our Father will provide our needs according to the riches of his kingdom. God's eye is on the sparrow. God provides what we need and as humans, we must not worry about our material objects but rather concentrate on God and the mercies to come.

To me, the following words are sacred and one I find hard to do on occasion. The human nature of the beast contains arrogance, pride, hate, and vengeance. Yet here again Christ directs us on the path. *'And forgive us our trespasses, as we forgive those who trespass against us.'* Trespass means to err or to sin. It is making an unwarranted or uninvited incursion on another. It is being hurtful or disrespectful. We are taught to pray for one another and forgive freely. We must forgive, as God forgives us when we earnestly seek that forgiveness.

'And lead us not into temptation but deliver us from evil.' Here Christ is showing us how to ask for Divine strength. He shows us how to pray for forte of spirit in defeating sin and how to resist the devil. He provides us, as God's children, an entreaty that will sustain us, guide us, and make us better followers of our God.

In the last section of the prayer, Jesus is closing it as he opened it. He is praising His/Our Father. Listen to the words. *'For thine is the kingdom, and the power, and the glory, forever and ever.'* Jesus is letting His/Our Father know that all thing belongs to God. We are reaffirming our belief that God is the provider. That God is the Creator of all things and that His kingdom is above all things on this earth.

Jesus ends with one powerful word: *'Amen'*. This is a way of saying, "So be it, truly, so it is, verily". The word is reiterating and confirming that what has been said is the truth. So, the Lord's Prayer taught to us by Jesus Christ is proclaimed with the last word in it as the eternal truth.

Friend, I ask you to do something. I ask you to read the words given to us by our God and our savior Jesus Christ. I ask you to read them not with your mind but rather with your soul. I ask you to take them to your heart and ponder upon the seventy words that will not only guide you but lead you to the King of Kings and Lord of Lords. We call Him, *'Our Father'*.

"Our Father which art in heaven, Hallowed be thy name. Thy kingdom come. Thy will be done in earth as it is in heaven. Give us this day our daily bread. And forgive us our trespasses, as we forgive those who trespass against us And lead us not into temptation, but deliver us from evil: For thine is the kingdom, and the power, and the glory, forever and ever. Amen." Matthew 6: 9-13

FROM THE CRADLE TO THE GRAVE

There is a saying that rings so true. It goes, *"What the mother sings to the cradle goes all the way to the grave."* I can't recall the first time I was taught this simple lesson. but it has been ingrained within the confines of my spirit for all these years. I can remember in my childhood a precious memory. Just before going to bed, I knelt with my hands on the mattress, placed my hands together in a sign of worship, and repeated the following words: *"Now I lay me down to sleep. I pray the Lord my soul to keep. If I die before I wake, I pray the Lord my soul to take."* I ended it in 'amen' and then got tucked into my little twin bed that was located in a two room long-house style log cabin deep within the shadows of the whispering pines of northern Michigan. I can still see mother's smile as she kissed my forehead.

Such small incidents like this are to be cherished. I remember my little girl and boy kneeling at the bed and saying their prayers. Those moments will never leave my soul. I only wish I had the ability to have been consistent with my children in teaching them and being an example. There is another old saying that I love. *"Treasure each other in the recognition that you will not always have one another."*

Jesus knew this very well. He stated in Matthew 26:11, *"For ye have the poor always with you but me ye have not always."* The disciples couldn't grasp that His time was limited and that He offered them by example and words, how to live. Only after He was gone, and the spirit descended upon them did they fully understand the need to teach others about prayer, salvation and how to live in, and abide in Christ.

I never did thank my mother for teaching me that simple prayer. I never did thank her for teaching me the importance of prayer. For you see in my youth, I thought everything would remain the same. I did not understand that one day, I would be a parent and have the wondrous responsibility of passing the torch of truth to my little ones. My only pray is that they remember enough of those moments to pass the childhood prayer of their father to my children's children...More importantly, this man prays that they provide a firm foundation, based on God's love to their cherubs, as my children follow Christ in their walk. Maybe then my morning song will contain the voice of my mother, once more singing me to sleep, and touching those she loved so unconditionally.

THE MAN BEHIND THE PLOW

I never met the man. My mother only knew of him what she was told by her mother, older siblings, aunts, and uncles. Yet he lingers. He was the man behind the plow.

It was a simpler time back then. It was a time when you earned a living by the sweat of your brow. You got up before the crack of dawn, and after working twelve hours in the mine, you came home exhausted. Every ounce of energy was given to providing and raising your family. There were hardly any frills or modern-day conveniences. Yet there was an abundance of love.

He was a simple man of the mountains. He was quiet and rarely raised his voice. He was a humble man of faith. His hands were calloused and rough as sandpaper. His body weathered by the years of hard work. His possessions were meager and his dwelling upon that mountain was scanty in nature. But the house had a sense of family beyond most. There was a sense of pride as well.

I was told that he worked in the mines. He got up early and prepared for his daily labor. His wife packed his lunch which usually consisted of a couple cat head biscuits, bologna, soup beans, cornbread, and an onion head. She would pack an occasional apple when they were in season. The old black dinner bucket was closed and the mason jar of sweet milk from their cow, so he could have his daily cornbread crumbled in his milk dessert.

She had the old carbide lamp laying on the kitchen table alongside of his mining hat. She waited until he was ready to leave and walked him outside. While she was preparing his lunch, he drew water from the well and filled the buckets that were on the porch. He checked to see that the boys had filled the coal buckets, so their mother wouldn't run out of coal for the cook stove and fireplaces. He left instructions for the oldest and expected the chores to be completed upon his return. He was never disappointed.

It was always dark when he left. He had an unusual way of walking. He never swung his arms but rather had them clasped behind his back. His pace was slow but steady. His lunch bucket was strapped to his side along with his mason jar. He had to walk down the old path with the carbide lamp as his only means of navigating in the darkness. On occasion, the moon would shed some light on the narrow path. He walked out of the holler, cross the old swinging bridge, and then walked the railroad for over two miles to portal where he worked.

He entered the mine with his fellow workers. Most of them had walked through the hills on what they called buffalo trails or Indian paths. Sometimes a shortcut across a mountain would be the shortest distance to work.

Sometimes they were able to ride in the buggy pulled by the mining mules. Other times they had to navigate down the dark shafted corridor and then begin their laborious task of loading coal. The work was hard. The dust from the mines filled their lungs but they knew they had to work to support their families. It was just the way it was.

After working a twelve-hour shift, he exited the mine and once again walked towards his home. The four-mile trip always seemed longer because of his exhaustion but he knew he had to get home to make sure everything was all right. The coal dust blackened his face as were his clothes. His carbide lamp once again befriended him on his pilgrimage home.

When he arrived, his faithful wife had a galvanized tub filled with hot water waiting for him on the porch. There he took off his clothes and bathed. Sometimes his wife would have to help wash his body because he was so sore or tired. It was a labor of love and she felt it was the least she could do for all that he had done. Clean clothes that had been placed there by his wife hung on the bannisters.

After cleaning up, he went into the house and there was greeted by his eleven children. He held the youngest while the oldest boys talked about what all they had done. He asked if they had fed the cows, chickens, and had they slopped the hogs. He knew the answer before asking, but he also knew that in this manner he built responsibility and pride within his children. He asked the girls if they had helped sweep, mop, do dishes and assist their mother in her daily chores. The answer was always the same and his response was always a smile along with a nod of his head.

He talked to them around the fireplace about his day and some of the tales told by his fellow miners. They all laughed at his poorly told jokes and clung to every word. When it was bedtime, he and his wife tucked in the youngest in a makeshift crib and hugged each one of their children. The couple insisted that the children recite a prayer while they were kneeling by the three feather beds that were lying on the floor. The kerosene lanterns were extinguished, and the couple walked to their bedroom. There they shared conversations between husband and wife.

Every morning the routine continued through those winter days. Snow didn't stop him from going to work. Sleet didn't deter his journey. He knew that if he didn't work, there would be no script to buy staples for his family. He worked in order for them to live.

During the spring, he had more daylight and a little more time. Before going to work and he was in the fields with old Jake, the family mule. Jake was accustomed to his master's voice, and a slight tug on the right or left rein beckoned the old mule to Gee or Haw.

His oldest of the boys were usually at his side. Each had their duties and executed them with the precise directions and expectations of their father. The land had to be cleared, rocks piled up in a stack, ground plowed, furrowed deep, and seeds planted. He knew that without the gardens, without the cornfields; without the harvest, times would be harsh in the winter. He spent hours upon hours behind the plow. There were times that his hands had blood blisters that had to be popped. Still, he went to work.

When he didn't have to work on Sundays, he was up early helping his beloved wife. He helped her get things ready for the children. When it was time, he would go into their room and wake up by singing, beating on a pot, or jumping on one of the feather beds. Their children would come gather around that old plank table and get the best breakfast of the week! Since there weren't enough chairs, the oldest either stood to eat or ate out on the porch.

After breakfast and the dishes were washed, everyone got ready for church. They weren't asked if they wanted to go, it was an expectation. The children had fair to descent clothes thanks to the dad's labor and their mother's handiwork. She had a couple of Sunday-go-meeting dresses and one pair of dress shoes that she wore with pride. She always insisted that the girls go with a bonnet or something covering their hair. The boys usually wore blue jeans of overalls. Both parents insisted that whatever they wore had to be clean.

He never had a store-bought suit. His wardrobe consisted of bib overalls. Most of them were ragged and patched. He always had a nice flannel shirt that he wore along his newest looking overalls. He cleaned off his mining boots the best he could and wore them down the mountain.

The church was simple building that housed the local families of the area. The preacher was one of the few men that did not work in the mines. Most of the men either worked in the mines or around the mines. The woman folk were usually related either by birth or married into the family.

After a Biblical hell fire and damnation sermon, there would be a dinner on the grounds. The families brought a covered dish and ate together. Some of the best times were when they had a gathering at a cemetery and then eating together while visiting loved ones that had gone on to their reward.

As the years went by, his oldest boy took up the family trade of coal mining. Every morning he would do the same routine as his father. They left together and walked in the dark talking about the old farm, family, faith, and the importance of taking care of one another. The father enjoyed those walks and was so glad that his son worked beside of him. His oldest boy had become a man.

They entered that old portal number 3 in the wee hours of the morning but to them it didn't matter. They went to work in the dark and returned home at night. Rarely did they see daylight. And when they did, they were usually working in order to support the family.

The son was told to carry the caged canary. They walked bent over deep into the abyss. The father walked a few steps in front of his son and every so often checked the ceiling and support timbers. He wanted to be extra careful this day, as Christmas eve was upon them. With both of them working, this would be the best Christmas the family ever had. He smiled at the thought of how excited the girls would be with new dresses from the camp store and how the boys would enjoy new shoes. Most of all, his wife would be surprised to get that new ringer washing machine. Well, it wasn't new but the folks that owned it had taken good care of it. They gave him a good price of seven dollars and they would deliver it by sled on Christmas morn. He again smiled as he walked deeper into the portal.

For some reason, the man was leery of that section of the mine. There was a rumor that a big black man had died in that particular section years ago and miners were fearful, and a bit superstitious. All experienced miners knew the sounds and signs of the mines. He was no exception, but his son was new to the ways of miners.

The rumblings came from one of the timbers supporting the ceiling. He knew that a cave in could occur. The dust and small pieces of rocks falling were signs. To his horror, his son was walking right into the bulging timbers. He yelled as he ran towards his oldest son. With a mighty shove, he pushed his son backwards. At that second, the roof gave way and caught the man beneath tons of rocks and debris. There was nothing that his son could do except cry out his father's name.

The other miners recognized the sound of broken timber and falling rocks. They came as fast as they could. They dug swiftly and furiously but the man was gone. His son hovered over his father as he embraced the lifeless body of the man who had done so much for him and his siblings. He could not be contained with his grief as he repeated over and over that it should have been him buried beneath tons of rocks.

The men stayed with him trying to console his grief, along with theirs, but it proved to be fruitless. As they placed the man's lifeless body on the back of a mine mule, one of the workers said that, for some reason, seeing him with that mule reminded him of just how great a man he was. He worked hard, never drank or cursed and believed in God's will. He had an everlasting love for his family and showed it every day through his time with his family, attending church, his work in the mines, and the countless hours he spent working the fields.

For some odd reason, those words touched the son's heart and helped ease the pain of his loss. Oh, he still grieved and suffered, as did the family, but he also realized that his father died as he lived. He died loving and following his sacred principles that he said he was duty bound to maintain. He died so his son would live. He followed the words of Jesus. He followed the deed of Jesus. For he followed the teachings of Christ in John 15:13 which states, "Greater love hath no man than this, that a man lay down his life for his friends."

He was a simple man, a quiet man. A man that followed the cross. He was a man that gave all for those he loved. He was the man behind the plow.

THE MAN BEHIND THE PLOW

He was a simple man.
A quiet man:
Soft as a kitten's meow.
He had calloused hands,
Yet loving hands.
That man behind the plow.

He was up before dawn
And had all the water drawn.
Even fed the old sow.
He went out in the fields
With a straw-hat for a shield:
That man behind the plow.

Though he weren't able,
He put food on the table,
And made ends meet somehow.
He was so humble, yet proud
He stood out in a crowd.
That man behind the plow.

No Sunday go meeting clothes.
He wore overalls with holes.
He lived by the sweat of his brow.
But when he went to his knees
God surely heard his pleas,
From that man behind the plow.

There was no running water
For his sons and his daughters
But they had milk from their cow.
Yes, they were threadbare
But love was always found there.
From that man behind the plow.

Those times have ended
But once we were befriended
By a man with sweat on his brow.
Though he is gone
His love lingers on
That man behind the plow.

Note: The Man Behind the Plow is dedicated to
my grandfather, Jim Blair, who on December 23,

1931, while working deep within the mines, he heard the rumblings of falling rock and timber. He ran and pushed his oldest son, Charlie Blair, out of harm's way. He saved my Uncle Charlie by giving his life. To me he is a hero. The mine was called Tea Pot and was located in Carbon Glow. Someday I will put a memorial stone at the mouth of that Portal Number 9 honoring the Man Behind the Plow. (John 15:13)

DADDY'S GIRL

Has it really been that long? Seems like only yesterday. I can recall every second of the event that I consider to be the scariest, yet one of the proudest of my life.

I remember when I was told about you. We were living in the 'blue zoo' at Morehead State University when your mother came in and announced that she was with child. I have never felt such a feeling. It was a mixture of fear, worry, excitement to the point of euphoria and a pervasive 'wondering' if everything was all right. Each day as I watched you push and kick, I gawked in wonder, I smiled, I worried, and, yes, I was scared. How could this miracle be? All I could do was pray that you would be healthy and that the first thing I would do would be to count your finger and toes! That shows my 'maturity' level of a father's first child.

I remember one time when your mother fell on the steps and had a big bruise on her stomach. That evening and night I don't remember ever praying so hard. I prayed for you to be spared of any damage, any hurt, any pain and that I would gladly take the injury for you. The good Lord heard my prayers and you got a clean bill of health.

I recall you insisting on being born and the mad rush I made in that 1972 Nova. It was painted metallic blue with a white top. That day it became my private jet. I made it to the hospital, registered, went upstairs, where the doctor tried to calm me down, as he prepped your mother. That was my most terrifying time. My first child was about to be born.

I remember walking back and forth, gently rubbing you through your mother's stomach, and trying to keep all the Lamaze steps down in my mind. I must have gone to the bathroom a dozen times! I paced back in forth and finally someone said for me to go get a pop to drink. I now realize that was a ploy to get me out of the room.

I went to the gift shop and remember buying a little stuffed animal. It was pink! I returned and the task of you entering into the world continued. I recall sweat running down my forehead and going to the bathroom to wipe it along with my hands.

Then came the final push and before my eyes was the most beautiful thing I had ever seen. I felt a tad faint when I was asked to cut the cord, but one look at your little wrinkled red face, watching your bottom jaw quiver, seeing all ten fingers and toes, and realizing that you had arrived, gave me the courage to do what was needed. I remember the silliest thing. Just before cutting the umbilical cord, I closed my eyes.

I wanted to protest when they took you away and cleaned you but knew it was in your best interest. Besides, we had to move to another 'guest' room. It seemed like years before you came back. Then the crowning moment of you being brought back into the room. When they handed you to me, I was overwhelmed! I tried to hide the tears from those in the room and, as silly as it sounds, didn't want the teardrops to fall on you (I think I was afraid you would drown!). For the longest time I looked into heaven's gates, as I held this little piece of heaven. I thought to myself, 'So this was what it feels like to bring life into the world.' That sensation has never left me nor will it ever.

Now you are grown, have a family of your own and though I rarely get to see you, in my heart and mind's eye, you linger. I talk to you and share things I do constantly. I no longer think of all those mistakes I made as a father. I no longer dwell on all the disappointments that gave you. I no longer think about what might have been. I no longer recall the saying that a child brings the greatest joys and the deepest sorrows. I no longer feel or remember anything other than love. The Bible states it best in Jeremiah 31:3: "I have loved you with an everlasting love." I thank God for those moments of yesterday. Therein, I shall be content. Unconditional love, that passes all understanding, abides within our souls; for the greatest of all things is love. And as I get ever closer to crossing through that turbid veil, I am even more convinced that someday we will once again walk hand in hand to the waterfalls, when daddy had a little girl. Happy Birthday daughter. Daddy loves you.

TREASURE IN A FRUIT JAR

Some of them were tinted blue. Others were clear glass. Some were Masons and others were Ball. Mother treasured them like they were golden. They were what she called 'fruit jars' or 'canning jars'. Within the confine of their shape were some of the best eating one can imagine.

She canned corn and sometimes pickled it. She made a special recipe of 'chow chow' handed down from her mother's mother. I took the mixture for granted, but now I'd give anything for just one more jar to mix with my soup beans. Beets were canned over my objections. Strangely enough, in my golden years, I have grown quite fond of them! Mother always canned beans and like magic, she would predict when the lid would seal while boiling. When strawberries were ripe, I would go pick them, clean them and then she'd can those sweet morsels to perfection. We picked blackberries, raspberries from our vines and can them as well. Apples, pears, and peaches were also her specialties. There were so many other things she canned.

One thing that sticks in my mind was her canned cabbage and sauerkraut. The reason I recall it so vividly was due to my daughter being a sauerkraut addict! She would get her mamma to open a jar and fry it. That little girl could eat a whole quart jar of kraut in one setting! I think she took that after me! I always loved it fried and then pile it on a hamburger with mother's canned pickles on top.

It was usually in the winter and towards the end of the month when we ate from the fruit jars. Mother would tell me to go get a jar of corn or beans. She always put the date she canned them on top of the lid with 'freezer tape'. It was the day they were preserved. I knew exactly which home canned items to get from the shelf because of the clear glass, date, and shape of its contents. The vessels containing the food were not what was important but was treated with respect. After the contents were emptied, the 'fruit jars' were washed out in that old tub under the pear tree, and later boiled so they would be sterilized.

I remember keeping the fire going under the old wash tub and sitting listening to mother talk. She always said the container was no good unless the lid sealed. The goodness of the fruit or vegetables inside were dependent upon the proper seal. Often, I pondered those words and I think I figured out the symbolism.

The jar is the 'clay pot' representative of our bodies. The items within the jar, 'vessel', or 'clay pot' are of no value unless the seal of salvation properly covers it. Then and only then is the contents of the jar or 'clay pot' good and able to feed others. The date that mother used to write on the top of the jar is representative of the day of salvation.

"But we have this treasure in jars of clay to show that this all-surpassing power is from God and not from us. ⁸We are hard pressed on every side, but not crushed; perplexed, but not in despair; ⁹persecuted, but not abandoned; struck down, but not destroyed. ¹⁰We always carry around in our body the death of Jesus, so that the life of Jesus may also be revealed in our body. ¹¹For we who are alive are always being given over to death for Jesus' sake, so that his life may also be revealed in our mortal body. ¹²So then, death is at work in us, but life is at work in you." 2 Corinthians 4:7-12

GENTLE WHISPERS

On my daily walks to the waterfall above the cabin, I am privy to His presence. Sometimes when I am still, I feel the wind gently caress my cheek. The sun shines through the leaves and seem to dance upon the ground. The squirrels protest my presence with their chattering, but ever so slowly, they accept me. The buzzing of the insects sings to my spirit. The butterflies float on the air. The frogs' chorus permeates and echoes on the cliff line. The water cascading down the cliff and landing in a pool below soothes my mortal body. The Douglas Fir smiles down upon the scene. I am content, and all is right in my world.

Then, there are those sacred moments as well, when I feel a presence that I cannot see. There are moments when I hear a gentle whisper. For the longest time I didn't understand, nor did I know the one that spoke. Then I discovered that others before me have heard the same voice. A young shepherd boy heard it while in the fields tending his sheep. David said in Psalm 81:5 that, *"I hear this most gentle whisper from One I never guessed would speak to me."* (The Message) Elijah heard him in a whisper as well. *"After the earthquake came a fire, but the Lord was not in the fire, but after the fire came a gentle whisper."* (I Kings 19:12)

I know Him. My soul recognizes His whisper. When I raise my hands in praise, I feel Him deep within my soul. I know He lives. His voice calms the storms. His whispers heal as surely as a touch from my Master's Hands.

I discovered something that I thought was a secret. Well, dear friend, it is no secret what God can do. The answer to hearing His voice and feeling his peace that passes all understanding in fixed within the confines of the Bible. The secret is in being still and believing. The Book of Books tells us how to hear His whispers. *"Be still and know that I am God."* (Psalm 46:10)

Do you want to hear Him? He's whispering to your soul as you read these words. If you listen in the stillness, truly believe, and draw nigh unto Him, He will be there. *"Draw nigh to God, and he will draw nigh to you. Cleanse your hands, ye sinners; and purify your hearts, ye double minded."* (James 4:8) He will come to you, whispering words of wisdom.

UNEXPECTED BLESSINGS

"Many O Lord my God, are thy wonderful works which thou hast done, and thy thoughts which are to us-ward: they cannot be reckoned up in order unto thee: if I would declare and speak of them, they are more than can be numbered." Psalm 40:5

Blessings sometimes come when we least expect them, and in a location that we would never imagine. Yet, they are a blessing beyond compare.

It was a normal day and I was doing my usual routine of stopping and getting a cup of coffee. I just paid the cashier and as I turned, there she was. Upon seeing me, she ran into my arms and hugged me in the most genuine manner. For a long time, we embraced and my heartbeat with such joy. Here was a student that I had not seen in years, yet she remembered me.

We talked for the longest time and she said that her life was completely turned around for the better. In fact, she told me that she and her husband were attending church and drove two hours just to be there for services. She recalled how I and others had touched her life and that she was recovering for addictions and had been free of the devil's grip for a long period.

I was overjoyed. We did share the loss of another student who fell into the devil's lair and how it had impacted both of us. The loss of a friend, student and human is always so sad, especially knowing the human potential whose ember has been extinguished. We talked about her family and how things had changed. I jokingly stated that I didn't have a gray hair on my head until I taught her. She laughed and said it was probably true. I told her how proud I was of her and that she was a success story. She wholeheartedly agreed. She said I had been a blessing to her and her family. She went on and stated that all the sickness of addiction was gone, and that God was doing for her what she could not do for herself. I smiled because that was my words I used to say. I reciprocated by saying she had been more of a blessing to me. In fact, she will never know the impact she and her siblings had on me.

I asked about her husband and she said he was in the car. After another hug, I excused myself but not without hearing and saying I love you. I then went out and talked to him. He always greets me with a firm handshake and smile. He said they were doing well and so were the kids. For a second, my mind flashed back to the time I talked about my children with such pride. We talked, and I invited him to an event. He said he would try to attend. I said my goodbyes and left feeling like my encounter was to lift my spirit with an unexpected blessing. In fact, I thought the meeting might have been an angel unaware.

Friends, the Bible has sixty-eight verses regarding blessings. Numbers 6:24-26 comes to mind. *"The Lord bless you and keep you; the Lord make his face shine on you and be gracious to you; the Lord turn his face toward you and give you peace."* Also, in Exodus 23-25, God tells us to: *"Worship the Lord your God, and his blessing will be on your food and water. I will take away sickness from among you."*

Friends, I ask you to note your encounters and see how many blessings you have. They are there, right in front of you. The time you narrowly escaped being hit by a car. The cashier who smiled at you and stated for you to have a good day. The man at a fast food restaurant who begins talking to you and sharing with you his family. They are out there for us. Just count them.

Johnston Oatman captured the message in song. In 1897, he published Count Your Blessings. *"Count your blessings, name them one by one, count your many blessings and see what God has done."*

LEAD ME TO THE ROCK

"The name of the Lord is a strong tower; the righteous run to it and are safe." Proverbs 18:10

Have you ever felt overwhelmed? Have you ever reached the point in which the very ground beneath your feet seems to be sinking sand? Does the daily stress weaken your resolve? Are you searching for answers to these nagging questions? I have good news!

There is a rock that is solid. There is a grace that is amazing. There is salvation found in sincere surrender! There is a way. There is a rock of ages.

Friend, sometimes we allow our morning song to be a mourning song. We allow the positives to be overrun by the negatives. God promised us an abundance of life, as well as love. In Matthew 6:33, Jesus said to seek God's Kingdom first and then see what happens. Here are His words! *"But seek ye first the kingdom of God, and his righteousness; and ALL these things shall be added unto you."*

We are not to lean upon our own understanding but rather, we are to trust in God. Don't believe me, well my friend read Proverbs 3:5. He wants us to have abundance of life (John 10:10) but in order to have it, you must seek out the Rock of Ages and surrender all.

An artist and songwriter by the name of Paul Baloche has written numerous contemporary gospel songs. They have been recorded by such artists as Casting Crowns, and Michal W. Smith. He has won several Dove Awards for his music. One of his songs captures the very essence of why we need the rock in our lives.

When my heart is overwhelmed, and my eyes are blind to You And the pain of life is just too heavy to bear and then the mountains seems so high and my faith's too weak to climb, Lead me to the rock that is higher than I (Refrain)

Lead me to the rock, lead me to the rock Lead me to the rock that is higher than I Lead me to the rock, lead me to the rock Lead me to the rock that is higher than I When my life is hit with fear And I fight to hide the tears And I wrestle in my heart to know what to do Lord, I'm welling up inside But I know You hear my cry Jesus, lead me to the rock that is higher than I.

You are the rock and there is no other A tower of strength, You are my shelter Lord, You are my hope eternal You are the rock that is higher than I. (Refrain)

There is also an old hymn published in 1896, that was written by Judson W. Van DeVenter. His hymn continues to bring forth a harvest of souls. His words exemplify that sweet surrender.

All to Jesus I surrender, All to him I freely give; I will ever love and trust him, In his presence daily live. (Refrain)

I surrender all, I surrender all, All to thee, my blessed Savior, I surrender all.

All to Jesus I surrender, Humbly at his feet I bow, Worldly pleasures all forsaken, Take me, Jesus, take me now. (Refrain)

All to Jesus I surrender; Make me, Savior, wholly thine; Let me feel the Holy Spirit, Truly know that thou art mine. (Refrain)

All to Jesus I surrender, Lord, I give myself to thee, Fill me with thy love and power, Let thy blessing fall on me. (Refrain)

All to Jesus I surrender; Now I feel the sacred flame. Oh, the joy of full salvation! Glory, glory, to his name! (Refrain)

This day; this hour, this very moment, surrender. Once you are led to the Rock, He will become your strength, your refuge, and your hope. Softly and tenderly, Jesus is calling. Let this day be your day to find the Rock.

AN EXPECTED END

"For I know the thoughts that I think toward you, saith the LORD, thoughts of peace, and not of evil, to give you an expected end." Jeremiah 29:11

We ae children of promise. We are promised prosperity as faithful Christians. It might not be in tangibles but friend, it is a guarantee that we will prosper while standing on the promises of God.

When God stated that He knew the plans He has for you, He is not joking. He knew you before you were born. He knew what would happen to the Israelites. He is all knowing and all powerful. He has plans for your life. BUT He also gives you freedom of choice. He guides you, via prayer and meditation, but the ultimate decision belongs to you. Isn't He wonderful?!

He offers thoughts of peace, filled with hope and a future. Being a follower of Christ and attempting to be a faithful servant, your future is bright. Oh, there will be temptations. There will be setbacks and even back sliding. But even with broken dreams, He is waiting on you with impending hope. He believes in you much, much more than you believe in yourself, and yes, even Him.

There is an old song that rings so true. Russell K. Carter wrote it and the song was published in 1886.

Standing on the promises of Christ my King, through eternal ages let his praises ring; glory in the highest, I will shout and sing, standing on the promises of God.

Standing, standing, standing on the promises of Christ my Savior; standing, standing, I'm standing on the promises of God.

Standing on the promises that cannot fail, when the howling storms of doubt and fear assail, by the living Word of God I shall prevail, standing on the promises of God. (Refrain)

Standing on the promises of Christ the Lord, bound to him eternally by love's strong cord, overcoming daily with the Spirit's sword, standing on the promises of God. (Refrain)

Standing on the promises I cannot fall, listening every moment to the Spirit's call, resting in my Savior as my all in all, standing on the promises of God. (Refrain)

Friend this is my morning song and it erases my mourning song. May you feel His presence and let it be your expected end.

AMERICA'S PREACHER

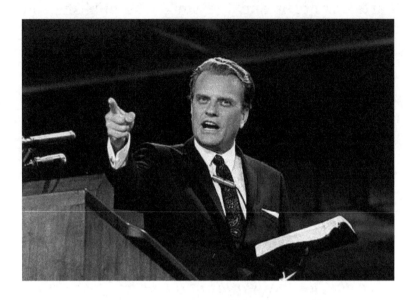

"My one purpose in life is to help people find a personal relationship with God, which, I believe, comes through knowing Christ."

On February 21, 2018, I awakened in my usual manner. I began getting prepared for the day and listening for my morning song. On this day I heard the words in my mind singing, "It is well with my soul," I took care of my morning chores and then decided to turn on the television. I couldn't believe the news; for on this day, I learned of the passing of America's preacher.

I never met the man but knew him as a child. I saw him on television and marveled at his eloquence in preaching. I witnessed thousands coming for huge auditoriums when the altar call was given. I recall my own personal experience as a child of eight. I touched the television, professed my sins at an altar call given by Reverend Graham. I loved him like a father.

At first, I wanted to mourn but then I thought of him and the reward he had earned. Not by words or deeds, but rather by his accepting Christ Jesus as his personal Savior. I recall a television interview when he was asked how he wanted to be remembered. He stated that all his hopes were in the hope that Jesus would remember him and simply say, "Well done thy good and faithful servant." What a testimony of faith.

He was a man of wisdom and his sayings still stir my soul. One of my favorite is, *"The thing that kept Christ on the cross was love, not a nail."* Oh, how very true. Another quote that moved my soul is, *"Mountaintops are for views and inspiration, but fruit is grown in the valleys."*

Somewhere along the way, I jotted down a saying by Reverend Graham on courage. I tried to life by that but failed on many occasions to do so. *"Courage is contagious. When a brave man stands, the spines of others are stiffened."*

Then I found one of Reverend Graham's sayings that's assisted me in my writings about life, for life

One, which struck a chord in my heart: *"We cannot truly face life until we face the fact that it will be taken away from us."*

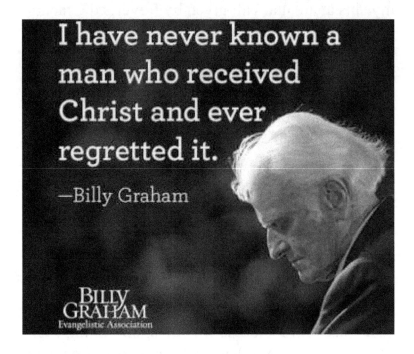

I have never known a man who received Christ and ever regretted it.
—Billy Graham

BILLY GRAHAM
Evangelistic Association

Here was a man who brought millions to Jesus, preached in over 185 countries, built a worldwide ministry, shared the gospel for over seventy+ years, yet was so humble in his reflections of his life's work.

Truly this man was God's servant. Truly this man showed us how to follow Christ. Truly this man followed the Christian path. Surely this man will hear the words he longed to hear: *"Well done thy good and faithful servant."*

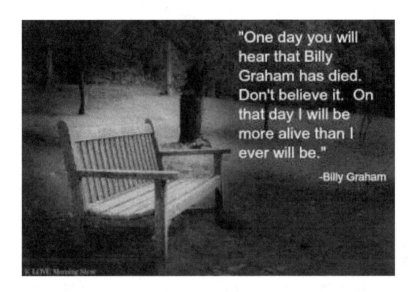

"One day you will hear that Billy Graham has died. Don't believe it. On that day I will be more alive than I ever will be."

-Billy Graham

DIVIDED HEART

"So then because thou art lukewarm, and neither cold nor hot, I will spue thee out of my mouth."
Revelation 3:16

In my life I have had so many opportunities to serve God. Unfortunately, I have led several of those chances slip by the wayside. There were times that I was doubleminded, trying to serve two masters. I remember my first time when my heart was divided.

I was a freshman in college and always had been interested in Christ's teachings. In fact, my plans were not to become a teacher, but rather, to become a preacher. I went to the library and checked out a book about the life of Christ. I remember lying on my bed reading it when some of my classmates came to ask me to go someplace. I said I was reading and one of them started making comments that were not Christian in nature. In fact, I was shocked to hear him making fun of me and my choice of literature. There was opportunity at that moment to witness but I chose the route of Peter and though I didn't deny Christ, I did laugh it off and went with them.

Another incident happened many years later. I was involved in an organization that I loved and one of the things I did as leader was to ask for our elected lay chaplain not only to offer an invocation but also offer a brief lesson/sermon. One day while visiting a friend, he said that a few of the men had been talking about the agenda. Then out of the blue he said, "If we wanted to go hear preaching, we would go to church on Sunday." That stunned me, yet I said nothing.

The longer I tried to guide the flock, the more I realized that I had to wash my hands of the group. I think they were glad to see me depart. I often regretted that I did not say or do something to defend the chaplain's moments.

I have however started standing my ground and refusing to bow to the powers that be in a secular world. I often ask those that I speak to that begin to grumble, if they are willing to set through a football game without moving, surely, they can maintain a level of interest through a service. I am becoming bolder in Christ while doing my best to remain humble in spirit.

Friends, one cannot live with a divided heart. The Bible tells me that if I grow closer to God, He will grow closer to me! (James 4:8). The Bible shows me that I cannot love the things of the world but rather must love the father.

Friends let us be in one accord. We worship the God of Abraham, the God of Creation, and the one and only God of ancient armies. This is our mission. This is our calling. As Jesus taught us, we must do with our whole heart. *"Thou shalt love the Lord thy God with all thy heart, and with all thy soul, and with all thy mind."* (Matthew 22:37) We must not lean on our own understanding but trust in God with our whole heart. (Proverbs 3:5)

This day let us pledge our allegiance to our God and mend the divided heart that beats within us. Let us earnestly seek God's guidance and ask Him to heal our broken hearts. And once we are strengthened, let us be like Peter and boldly proclaim the gospel of Jesus Christ to all.

"Being a double-minded man, unstable in all his ways." James 1:8

"No one can serve two masters; for either he will hate the one and love the other, or he will be devoted to one and despise the other You cannot serve God and wealth." Matthew 6:24

"You adulteresses, do you not know that friendship with the world is hostility toward God? Therefore, whoever wishes to be a friend of the world makes himself an enemy of God." James 4:4

HOW GREAT THOU ART

The other night, I was surfing the net and happened upon Vince Gill. He had some young people in his house and was showing them his guitars. He handed one to a young man and then he got one. He began to play, and a lovely young lady began singing one of my favorite songs. The song was How Great Thou Art. I was mesmerized. Then I found Carrie Underwood and Vince Gills rendition of the song. My heart overflowed with the spirit.

After the tributes to God ended (along with my tears of worship) I decided to discover the person who wrote such an inspirational song. The year was 1885 and the setting was in Sweden. Carl Bob erg, a lay parson, and sailor wrote it on one Sunday. The story goes like this.

As Carl was walking home from church service with some friends, he heard the church bells ringing. The colors of the earth were ripe, and his spirit was uplifted. Suddenly a fierce storm came from out of nowhere and just as suddenly, it subsided. A rainbow appeared in the heavens.

Carl went home and noted the Bay of Monsters from his window. He heard the sounds of birds in the distance. He sat down and wrote a poem capturing that moment. His son later stated that the poem was based on the eighth Psalm, which says in verse one-nine, *"Oh Lord our Lord, how excellent is thy name in all the earth who hast set thy glory above the heavens. Out of the mouth of babes and suckling's hast thou ordained strength because of thine enemies that thou still the enemy and the avenger. When I consider thy heavens, the work of thy fingers, the moon, and the stars, which thou hast ordained; what is man that thou art mindful of him? And the son of man that thou visitest him? For thou hast made him a little lower than the angels, and hast crowned him with glory and honor. Thou madest him to have dominion over the works of thy hands; thou hast put all things under his feet: all sheep and the beasts of the fields; the fowl of the air and the fish of the sea. And whatsoever passeth through the paths of the seas. O Lord our Lord, how excellent is thy name in all the earth!"*

But our loving Father wasn't finished with inspiring others to take this song and make it known throughout the world! In 1907, his poem was translated into German. In 1912, it was translated to Russian. Then in 1925, Gustav Johnson wrote the English version. 1931, Stuart Hine, while a missionary in the Ukraine, re-wrote portions of the song and gave it the title, How Great Thou Art. Finally, Hine published two additional verses in 1953. With Billy Graham's crusades, the song, as sung by George B. Shea, began internationally known. It was also the theme song to Billy Graham's radio show. To this day it is only second to Amazing Grace in terms of being endeared to worship services. Such is the power of inspiration at God's wonders!

Friends, does your soul sing? Do you know just how great He is? Listen to the thunder! Hear the chirping of the morning birds and their morning song. Look unto the mountains or cast your eyes upon His seas. Gaze upon the beauty of His creations! Then think of His sacrifice upon the cross so that we can join Him in a utopia beyond our wildest imaginings. It is then you will proclaim, How Great Thou Art!

Lyrics to How Great Thou Art

O Lord my God, when I in awesome wonder,
Consider all the worlds Thy hands have made;
I see the stars, I hear the rolling thunder,
Thy power throughout the universe displayed.
Chorus:

Then sings my soul, my Savior God, to Thee,
How great Thou art! How great Thou art!
Then sings my soul, My Savior God, to Thee,
How great Thou art! How great Thou art!
When through the woods, and forest glades I

wander,
And hear the birds sing sweetly in the trees.
When I look down, from lofty mountain grandeur
And hear the brook, and feel the gentle breeze.
Chorus

And when I think that God, His Son not sparing;
Sent Him to die, I scarce can take it in;
That on the cross, my burden gladly bearing,
He bled and died to take away my sin.
Chorus

When Christ shall come, with shout of
acclamation,
And take me home, what joy shall fill my heart.
Then shall I bow, in humble adoration,
And then proclaim, "My God, how great Thou
art!"

Resources

http://www.mannamusicinc.com/hgta.htm
http://www.christianitytoday.com/ct/2013/april-web-only/how-great-thou-art-100-year-old-bass.html
https://suite.io/tel-asiado/dnz23x
http://en.wikipedia.org/wiki/How_Great_Thou_Art
http://anokachurch.org/how-great-thou-art-story/
https://www.crosswalk.com/faith/spiritual-life/the-story-you-don-t-know-behind-how-great-thou-art.html

HELL FOR CERTAIN

"But I will forewarn you whom ye shall fear: Fear him, which after he hath killed hath power to cast into hell; yea, I say unto you, Fear him."
Luke 12:5

Years ago, I had the honor of teaching college classes in Hyden, which is located in Leslie County, Kentucky. It was my first night class and I was a little nervous. As was my custom, I left home early to scout out the campus. I found the school and my room. I noted that I had time to grab a bite to eat and there was a Dairy Queen just down the road. So, I went there.

I ordered my food and sat down at a table. Across from me was an elderly man in bib overhauls and a straw hat. He was eating when I sat down. I nodded at him in recognition and he reciprocated. I continued eating and noted that the elderly gentleman was emptying his tray. A younger man came in and greeted the elder. They talked a little and then the young man asked him where he was headed.

The old man grinned and simply said, *"Going to hell for certain."*

My eyes got bigger than watermelons! I thought to myself why on earth would anyone brag about going there?!

Without blinking, the younger man stated, *"I'll be there shortly."*

My jaw dropped, and I began wondering what condition these two men had. I emptied my tray and pondered the words I had heard while driving to the college. I parked my car at the high school and gathered my gear for class. I went into my room and wrote my usual outlines on the board.

My class began to assemble, and I greeted them at the door. When it was time to begin, I introduced myself, spoke of the class and in an effort to get to know them better, I gave each one a student survey. The survey asked such items as name, address, phone number, major, five things about him or herself and what did they expect out of the class. I gave them time to answer the survey, and as was my custom, used it to associate names with faces.

As I called the student's names I began to read addresses that were different, to say the least! Thousand Sticks was one that sparked my curiosity. I asked the class and they said it was named after a creek that flowed close to the toll booth off the Daniel Boone Parkway (renamed Hal

Rogers Parkway). I asked why it was called that and someone stated it was named by the pioneers. The creek was said to have so many stumps sticking up like sticks, that they called it Thousand Sticks. Interesting!

I found an address called Cutshin. I inquired about it and once again a student stated that it was named by a frontiersman or traveler who cut his shin while crossing a creek. Then I picked up another student and smiled at the address: 'Hell for Certain'. I laughed inwardly, realizing that the old man was indeed going to 'Hell for Certain'. That was where he must live! Well, that name peaked my interest.

I asked about how that place received its name. One of the students said it was also known as Dry Hill but most folks called it by the former name. Another went on and said that a long time ago, preacher went through the area. When he returned to his area, he was asked where he went. The preacher answered he didn't know but it was hell for certain! The name stuck.

After I became familiar with the people and the area, I found them to be most hospitable and God fearing. They greeted me with a smile and always treated me with such kindness. But there was a lesson for me during that brief encounter with the fine old farmer.

Friends, the Bible speaks of hell. Jesus preached more about the fire and brimstone of hell than any other topic. We are warned of eternal damnation, yet some people act like they don't care if they go there. Hell is for certain UNLESS you are washed in the blood of Jesus Christ. Friends, you will go there if you have not earnestly repented of your sins, asked God to forgive you and surrender yourself to Him.

I can honestly say I do not want to spend one second in hell and that is for certain! Though I am a chief sinner, my name is written in the book of life through Christ dying on the cross, raising on the 3rd day, and offering me a way into His kingdom. *"And whosoever was not found written in the book of life was cast into the lake of fire."* (Revelations 20:15) Did Jesus not state in Matthew 13:50 that He, *"Shall cast them into the furnace of fire: there shall be wailing and gnashing of teeth."*

The plan of salvation is so simple and what do you have to lose but your eternal soul? Think my friends, with the acceptance of Christ as your personal Savior, you forgo the torture of eternal burning, eternal pain and will not be cast asunder. BUT if you do not accept Him there is no doubt in this fielder's mind that you are going to 'hell for certain."

DO YOU KNOW ME?

It was a mundane day as I drove into the parking lot to get something to eat. I was in an 'OK' mood but was taking things for granted. All that changed when I was seated by the waitress.

I was placed in a booth and directly across from me was a well-dressed older Black gentleman. Our eyes met, I nodded and offered a typical good day greeting. He looked at me with hollow eyes and said, "Do you know me?" I said I did not but was just being cordial. He stared at me for a few seconds and then said, "Do you know where I am?" It was then that realization kicked in with the force of a mule's kick.

I stepped over to his table and asked him did he need any help. By then the manager came up to me and took me to the side. She said that he had wondered in and was disorientated. He didn't have an ID on him and he didn't know who he was or how he got there. I asked the gentleman did he have any keys and he handed me his jacket. We looked, and they were in the inside pocket of his coat.

We went out and pushed the alarm button. His car began honking and we went to it. The front and back seat was loaded with clothes, trash, and other debris. We sifted through it and found his cell phone. The manager called the contact number and when it rang, she explained the situation. The daughter was so relieved that I heard her crying as she shouted to someone, "They found daddy!"

She told the manager that the last she had heard from him was in Illinois. She said he had dementia and took spells where he didn't know anybody or what was going on around him. Apparently, he had drove away from his home and no one knew where he was. The daughter lived in South Carolina and said she would be there in about five or so hours. The manager reassured her that she and the staff would take good care of him.

We went back into the restaurant and sure enough the staff was around him, reassuring him and offering everything to eat. He nibbled but wanted to know who they were and who he was. My heart bent in submission to the overwhelming guilt I had for taking my mind and life for granted. Yet I felt such comfort seeing how the staff and manager nurtured this complete stranger.

They reassured me that the old gentleman would be all right and after I ate, I went on my way. I stopped at a store, but my mind was back at the restaurant. I knew he was in good hands, but for some reason, I just couldn't leave without knowing that his family had arrived and was going to take him home. After I did my errands, I went back.

I noted he was sitting in the same position and had his head on the table. The manager reassured me that he was fine and had eaten a few bites. I asked if I could just hang around and she said sure. I told her that I would buy any food he might eat but she just smiled, shook her head, and said, "It's taken care of". The look in her eyes and those waiting on the old man told me that I was in the presence of angels unaware.

Time went by and a van pulled up into the parking lot. A young lady bounded out of the car and ran into the restaurant. She saw her father and begin crying, "Daddy, Daddy" as she ran and embraced her lost father in an act of unconditional love. We all broke down crying at the site of the reunion. The manager introduced herself and through the tears, the family thanked all the staff. I stayed in the background because they truly were the heroes.

They gathered his things and left in deep gratitude. As they pulled out in the van and the old gentleman's car, I realized I didn't even know the names of these people. In fact, I left the restaurant without asking the manager or staffs' names. But that is not important, for I saw a true act of being a good Samaritan. I saw people give of themselves without thought of reward. I saw hope in a world too busy to notice those around them. I saw what love; true love looks like. I saw angels unaware. It seems that He keeps sending me angels to guide me and help me along my path.

The Bible tells us in James 2:15-17, *"Suppose you see a brother or sister who has no food or clothing, and you say, "Good-bye and have a good day; stay warm and eat well"—but then you don't give that person any food or clothing. What good does that do? So you see, faith by itself isn't enough. Unless it produces good deeds, it is dead and useless."* Job 29:11-12, cries out to His people to help others! *"Whoever heard me spoke well of me, and those who saw me commended me because I rescued the poor who cried for help, and the fatherless who had none to assist them."* Then there is Luke 10:25-37, where Christ teaches us how to be a good neighbor through the parable of the Good Samaritan.

Friend let us seek to be a little kinder, a little more understanding and a lot more loving to those we encounter. Does not our Lord and Savior tell us to, 'Love thy neighbor as thyself?' Remember, they may well be angels watching and testing our character when we think no one is observing. And the question the old gentleman asked me (Do you know me?) may well be Christ asking you the same.

A.R.K-BEGINNINGS

"And as ye would that men should do to you, do ye also to them likewise." Luke 6:31

A.R.K. Today I begin a journey and invite you to come along. It is called Act of Random Kindness. I share this in hopes that you will share with others YOUR ARK.

As I sat having my morning coffee at McDonalds, an elderly gentleman and his wife came in and ordered. HE was wearing a Marine cap and stooped over with age. They sat down across from me and when the food was brought to them, I noted they offered a prayer. I was touched to see an outward sign of an inward peace from this family. I went to my car and started to leave but the spirit stirred. I got out, opened my trunk, and picked up my book entitled UNSUNG HEROES, went back in, thanked him for his service, and presented the book to them. The look in his eyes was all the thanks I needed. Both were very appreciative.

I share this not for glory except to glorify God for giving us such American heroes. I share this to ask you to do a A.R.K. with no thought of reward for yourself. I ask you from this day forward to be a little kinder and a little less centered around your world. I ask you today to begin your A.R.K as a covenant between you and our Creator. I ask you to sing a morning song so that others will hear and know that He walks beside you. I ask you to walk in the shadow of the cross.

Friends, as we walk through this life, let us be more cognizant of the needs of others, for we do not know what they are experiencing in their lives. Jesus prayed for the poor, the infirmed, the lost souls, and the troubled. Can we not follow His example without seeking praise of others? Finally, I ask you to practice the following prayer: *"Help me to be, to think, to act what is right because it is right; make me truthful, honest, and honorable in all things; make me intellectually honest for the sake of right and honor and without thought of reward to me."*

I SAW TWO WOLVES

"Honor your father and your mother, as the LORD your God has commanded you, that your days may be prolonged and that it may go well with you on the land which the LORD your God gives you."
Deuteronomy 5:16

There is an old American Indian legend. It goes something like this. A grandson went to his grandfather to talk to the old sage. The grandson is troubled and sought advice. He told his grandfather that his spirit is disturbed. It was as if two wolves were within him. One was bright and filled with goodness. The other dark and occupied with hate. The grandson asked his wise grandfather which would win the fight for his heart. The old sage looked lovingly at his grandson and then spoke. "Grandson, it will be the one that you feed."

As I shopped for some items at a Walmart, my attention was drawn to a screaming child a couple isles away. Her loud piercing wails beckoned me, for I thought she might be injured. Upon arriving I noted a young girl of approximate nine years throwing a temper tantrum. Her parents were doing everything they could to end her displeasure, but she continued trashing around, cursing, and slapping at her father. Finally, the mother got the item creating the disruption and gave it to her. As sudden as the rage began, it stopped.

My first thought was *'The discontented child cries for toasted snow'* and those parents best get ready for another 'fit' when the child didn't get her way. Then I thought of what my mother would have done in that situation. I am sure a hand would have been placed on a part of my body to get my attention! But I also know that I would have never had dishonored my mother in such a manner due to my upbringing, respect and to be quite candid, fear! She always taught me and corrected me when needed. I recall her saying, *"Discipline is something you do For a child. Punishment is something you do TO a child."* That lesson stuck.

The same day, I was at a grocery store and noted a father with his child. He was talking and communicating with his offspring. As they walked the child asked if he could have something and the father shook his head. He explained why and asked did his son understand. The child shook his head in a fashion favoring yes and they went on. I noted a level of mutual respect and love. Often the father patted his child on the head and I overheard a reciprocal 'I love you' being sincerely given. I thought to myself that the parents of the little girl, as well as that child, could learn from this parent.

There is a saying that goes, *"What the mother sings at the cradle goes all the way to the grave."* I believe that to be inclusive of both parents. I also believe the Holy Bible when it tells us to honor our fathers and mothers. In Ephesians 6:2 we are instructed to, *"Honor your father and mother, which is the first commandment with a promise."*

As I think of the wolves I saw, I realized that if falls upon the parents to pass the lessons they learned from their parents to the rising generation. It pleased God to see the good wolf being taught. So, friends, let us continue to fight the dark wolf and chase him away from our children's souls by teaching them Godly principles we are duty bound to maintain.

"But if a widow has children or grandchildren, they must first learn to show godliness to their own family and repay their parents, for this is pleasing in the sight of God." 1 Timothy 5:4

THE BLESSING OF THE SWORD

(Mort Kuntsler: Blessing of the Sword)
{http://www.mortkunstler.com/}

"For the word of God is living and active, sharper than any two-edged sword, piercing to the division of soul and of spirit, of joints and of marrow, and discerning the thoughts and intentions of the heart." Hebrews 4:12

At one of the events I attended, I was asked to bless the sword. I felt unworthy to do so but having seen Father Anderson's moving blessing, I agreed to do so. As I researched it, I began to realize that the blessing was a very sacred ritual and it began with the Bible, which is considered to be the 'sacred sword' of wisdom, power, and love.

I searched for Bible verses and 'surfed' the internet for protocols. I found many, inclusive of the Knight's Templar's blessing. The blessing is quite lovely, and I share it for you to reflect upon the olden days of chivalry. *"Harken, we beseech Thee, O Lord, to our prayers, and deign to bless with the right hand of Thy Majesty this sword with which Thy servant wishes to be girded, that it may be a protection of churches, widows, orphans, and all Thy servants against the cruelty of pagans, and may it be the fear, terror and dread of all evil-doers. In the name of Christ the Lord. Amen."*

As I read it (and though excellent in context), I came to realize that this blessing was for their ritual and that I had to discovery one for the Civil War era. As I researched I came across Mort Kuntsler's marvelous painting depicting the 'Blessing of the Sword'. I read his comments about the blessings and upon gazing at his work, realized what I needed to write. I offer his words for clarity and understanding of the significance of the ceremony.

"Often such ceremonies were capped by the presentation of an ornately engraved edged weapon. It was offered with a heartfelt blessing - a leave-taking benediction of hope that the sword would remain sheathed or that it would provide protection from the brutality of battle. It was typically received with gratitude - and a vow to

carry it with honor, to faithfully do one's duty, to return when the homeland no longer needed defending - and even in the darkest hour to remember those left behind. Then the time of departure was at hand, the man in gray was gone - and the blessing of the sword remained only as a memory. The idea for this work was suggested to me several years ago, but I did not decide to paint it until I discovered this 19th century poem by T.B. Read." Mort Kuntsler

After reading his words and viewing his portrait of the blessing of the sword, after prayer, and beseeching God for words, I decided to write my own blessing incorporating key aspects of all the things I had read and seen. I included the poem that inspired Mr. Kuntsler's work, which is entitled, The Brave at Home.

Before the time of King David, the sword was a symbol of strength, valor, courage, hope, and honor. Today we recall those sacred principles and reaffirm our faith in maintaining them. The blessing of the sword offers hope that it may never be drawn, but if our sacred principles are tramped upon, it is the duty of the bearer to defend the homeland and the honor of our heritage. The defender must wear it with honor and faithfully execute his duties, being reminded of our knights of old, whose chivalrous nature must be carried forth with humbled pride and stand firm against the enemy of righteousness and our liberties.

The Bible speaks of the sword in many passages. In Ezekiel 21: 3-9, the Book of Books says, "Thus says the LORD, *"Behold, I am against you; and I will draw My sword out of its sheath and cut Because I will cut off from you the righteous off from you the righteous and the wicked. ⁴ and the wicked, therefore My sword will go forth from its sheath against all flesh from south to north. ⁵ Thus all flesh will know that I, the LORD, have drawn My sword out of its sheath. It will not return to its sheath again."'* ⁶ As for you, son of man, groan with breaking heart and bitter grief, groan in their sight. ⁷ And when they say to you, 'Why do you groan?' you shall say, *'Because of the news that is coming; and every heart will melt, all hands will be feeble, every spirit will faint and all knees will be weak as water. Behold, it comes and it will happen,'* declares the Lord GOD. Again, the word of the LORD came to me, saying, ⁹ "Son of man, prophesy and say, 'Thus says the LORD.' Say, *'A sword, a sword sharpened And also polished! 'Sharpened to make a slaughter, Polished to flash like lightning!'*

There is a poem, which was written in the 19ᵗʰ century, that summates the importance of having the sword blessed as well as the hope surrounding the rite. It was written by T.B. Read.

The Brave at Home

The wife who girds her husband's sword
'Mid little ones who weep or wonder,
And bravely speaks the cheering word,
Even though her heart be rent asunder,
Doomed nightly in her dreams to hear
The bolts of death around him rattle,
Has shed as sacred blood as e'er
Was poured upon the field of battle.

So, as in olden days, into your hands I place this sword sanctified by the mission. It is your solemn duty to carry it with pride and humbleness of heart, praying that it is never drawn in anger, but rather in defense of our homeland. Following the words of the Sacred Sword, which we call the Holy Bible, I hereby bless the sword and its bearer in the name of the Father, Son and Holy Spirit. Benedictus!

"Like a muddied spring or a polluted fountain is a righteous man who gives way before the wicked."
Proverbs 25:25

WADE IN THE WATER

"I baptize you with water for repentance, but he who is coming after me is mightier than I, whose sandals I am not worthy to carry. He will baptize you with the Holy Spirit and fire." Matthew 3:11

One of the greatest joys of my childhood was wading in the water. I recall wading across the shallow portion of Muskrat Lake and the numerous times I rode my bike to AuSable River below Red Oak to wade, splash and feel the water rushing past me. I used to love a heavy rain and couldn't hardly wait to go outside and play in the mud puddles.

When I moved to eastern Kentucky, I soon discovered the river. In those days, there wasn't a road in and out of the holler, so we had to either walk across the swinging bridge or wade the north fork of the Kentucky River. I always chose to wade when possible. Water seemed to have cast a magical spell on me.

It wasn't until later in life that I began to understand and appreciate the significance of water and the symbolism of 'wading in the water'. My first encounter came when I was told of Jesus wading in the water to be baptized. He set the example for us all. I recall the stories in the Bible of water returning sight to a blind man, healing a leper, and making a crippled man regain use of his legs. But it wasn't the water but rather what was IN the water. It is called faith! They believed in their hearts what Jesus said and trusted Him completely. Their faith via the symbol of baptism healed them.

I remember the first old Regular Baptist baptism I witnessed as a child. I admit I was scared at the singing and preaching. But when I saw I.D. Back and other elders of the church dunk that man and he came up shouting, I felt such astonishment. The water didn't purify the man but rather what was IN the water did. That symbolic act of cleansing made me realize years later that I too had to be submerged in order to symbolically take off the old coat and put on the new.

Jesus was without sin. He was pure. He was baptized to identify with us and to show us the way. As for me, I was and am a sinner. The only difference is I am now a saved sinner trying to do better. Did it change me for the better? I believe that I was the same sinner but covered by grace and faith in the cleaning of the water and now had an active conscience reminding me of my commitment and my surrender to the Almighty. Water baptism is a symbol of trust and reliance on Christ. I became a member of God's household (Ephesians 2:19)!

Romans 6:3-7 tells us that, *"Do you not know that all of us who have been baptized into Christ Jesus were baptized into his death? We were buried therefore with him by baptism into death, in order that, just as Christ was raised from the dead by the glory of the Father, we too might walk in* <u>*newness of life.*</u> *For if we have been united with him in a death like his, we shall certainly be united with him in a resurrection like his. We know that our old self was crucified with him in order that the body of sin might be brought to nothing, so that we would no longer be enslaved to sin. For one who has died has been set free from sin."*

Before His ministry, Jesus waded into the water. Then He began the journey and created a path for us to follow Him into eternity. Friend, He invites you to wade into the water and know the true meaning of love, peace, joy, and unabated fellowship when you walk with Him. Jesus is calling, oh sinner, come home. Step on in, don't be scared the water is fine. Come join Him and wade into the water.

HOW CAN I KEEP FROM SINGING?

The other day I stopped at my friend, Gwen's Antique Shop to visit. One of my lifelong friends was there. Every time we get together, there is laughter and shared memories. On this occasion she talked about a memorial service that was held and that she sang a song. She told me the title, but I didn't recognize it, so she sang the first verse.

As I listened to her soothing vocalization, an old memory crept into my mind. I had heard it, but the title had through me off track. After our visit, I went home and immediately looked up the song on the internet. It was then that I recall hearing it as a student at Calvary College. The title of the song is, How Can I Keep from Singing?

According to Wikipedia, the hymn was attributed to have been written by a Baptist minister named Robert Wadsworth Lowry. It was published on August 7, 1868. The words are electrifying and stirs this fielder's soul.

One verse in particular moved me to sing. It goes, "No storm can shake my inmost calm while to that Rock I'm clinging. Since love is Lord of heaven and earth, how can I keep from singing?"

For some reason only known to my immortal soul, chills run up and down my arms, shoulders and back whenever I think of this. A 'joyful noise' radiates from my heart and I find such peace in the silent song glorifying God. This must be the feeling that King David had when he wrote the songs of the Psalms. The King of Israel couldn't keep from singing! This must be what Christ meant when he told the Pharisees in Luke 19: 37-40, when the hypocrites wanted Jesus to stifle his disciples 'singing' *"Blessed is the king who comes in the name of the Lord. Peace in heaven and glory in the highest."* The disciples couldn't keep from singing! Then Christ said, *"I tell you if they keep quiet, the stones will cry out."*

Another line that lifts my heart to the heavens says, "All things are mine since He is mine!" How very true and when I ponder upon this, my soul sings, How Great Thou Art. Oh what a mighty God we have. He is the Alpha and Omega, the beginning, and the end. He is the one and only. He is the God who makes our spirits soar in song. He is the one who placed the songs in our hearts, so that we can praise Him as do the angels. How can we keep from singing?

How Can I Keep from Singing?

My life flows on in endless song,
above earth's lamentation.

I hear the clear, though far off hymn
that hails a new creation
Refrain:

No storm can shake my inmost calm
while to that Rock I'm clinging.
Since love is Lord of heaven and earth,
how can I keep from singing?

Through all the tumult and the strife,
I hear that music ringing.
It finds an echo in my soul.
How can I keep from singing?
(Refrain)

What though my joys and comforts die?
I know my Savior liveth.
What though the darkness gather round?
Songs in the night he giveth.
(Refrain)

The peace of Christ makes fresh my heart,
a fountain ever springing!
All things are mine since I am his!
How can I keep from singing?
(Refrain)

Source:

https://en.wikipedia.org/wiki/How_Can_I_Keep_fr
om_Singing%3F

JUST ACROSS THE RIVER

"Thou shalt no more be termed Forsaken; neither
shall thy land any more be termed Desolate; but
thou shalt be called Hephzibah and thy land
Beulah; for the LORD delighteth in thee, and thy
land shall be married."
Isaiah 62:4

Have you ever had a longing; a desire; a craving for something? Have you ever wondered what is just over the mountain, beyond the sea or on the other side of the sunset? Have you ever had a thirst for something but not sure what it was? Have you ever gone to the refrigerator with no iota of what you want to eat but still drawn to look and figure out what your body desires to eat?

This day my yearnings seemed to overwhelm me. Yet, it was something so sweet and so pure that I could not control my tears. It was a longing for Beulah Land.

One of my favorite singers is Jason Crabb. His vocalizations are truly a gift from God. I happened upon the song Beulah Land performed by him. As I listened to his rendition, tears flowed down my cheeks and my heart was lifted beyond the turbid veil unto the Most-High. There was a longing that I cannot explain. There was a feeling of satisfaction and complete peace that defies definition. There was a moment when I felt as if I was between two worlds hesitating.

After listening to the song several times, I decided to read about the song. I found it quite interesting. I also found the words to be so penitent, yet beautiful explicit. I found simplistic complexity within the words. Oh, how true are the words: "I'm kind of homesick for a country" and "I'm looking now, just across the river" Within the stanza is faith, hope, and charity.

Beulah Land

I'm kind of homesick for a country
To which I've never been before.
No sad goodbyes will there be spoken
For time won't matter anymore.

Beulah Land I'm longing for you
And some day on thee I'll stand
There my home shall be eternal
Beulah Land, sweet Beulah Land

I'm looking now, just across the river
To where my faith, shall end in sight
There's just a few more days to labor.
Then I will take my heavenly flight.

Beulah Land I'm longing for you
And some day on thee I'll stand

There my home shall be eternal
Beulah Land, sweet Beulah Land
Beulah Land, oh it's Beulah Land
Oh Beulah Land, sweet Beulah Land

The words to Beulah Land are attributed to Edgar Page Stites (1836-1921). Stites was from New Jersey. His genealogy shows that his ancestors were on the Mayflower. At nineteen years of age he was saved in what was known as the Awakening of 185-58, just two years before the War Between the States.

Edgar P. Stites described how he wrote the words and his emotions during the writing. Surely, he was merely the pen and God was the writer. *"It was in 1876 that I wrote 'Beulah Land.' I could write only two verses and the chorus, when I was overcome and fell on my face. That was one Sunday. On the following Sunday I wrote the third and fourth verses, and again I was so influenced by emotion that I could only pray and weep. The first time it was sung was at the regular Monday morning meeting of Methodists in Philadelphia. Bishop McCabe sang it to the assembled ministers. Since then it is known wherever religious people congregate. I have never received a cent for my songs. Perhaps that is why they have had such a wide popularity. I could not do work for the Master and receive pay for it."*

John R. Sweeney (1837-1899) put the lyrics to music in 1875. He was a camp song leader and must have been inspired by God as well. The end result is a song of the ages that has been sung and will be sung at different events, funerals, and revivals. Friend satisfy your longing, your hunger and thirst. Be ready to embrace Beulah Land.

"Blessed are those who hunger and thirst for righteousness, for they shall be satisfied."
Matthew 5:6

"My soul longs, yes, faints for the courts of the LORD; my heart and flesh sing for joy to the living God."
Psalm 84:2

Resources

https://en.wikipedia.org/wiki/Beulah_Land

http://www.faughnfamily.com/hymn-reflections-beulah-land/

videos/search?q=jason+crabb+sweet+beulah+land&docid=607990521887984541&mid=768F40876D1D3BEC803D768F40876D1D3BEC803D&view=detail&FORM=VIRE

A FATHER TO THE FATHERLESS

"A father to the fatherless, a defender of widows,
is God in his holy dwelling."
Psalm 68:5

As I read all the notes from children to their fathers wishing them a Happy Father's Day, I am taken back. I recall my father, that strong Greek immigrant who came to America to pursue the American dream. He came by ship across the Atlantic. He came with his older brother. Both were stowaways. Both came to get away from being indentured. Both came so they could do more than be a sheepherder.

I can only imagine the look of wonder in their eyes as they saw the Statue of Liberty. She embraced them, as she welcomed them to the land of opportunity. My father and Uncle Tom migrated to Detroit where they became dishwashers. Over the years they became chefs and ended up owning a couple of restaurants in Greektown. They were living their dream.

Mother was a waitress working for my father. She was quite younger than her, but love knows no age. They were married and before long, I entered their world. This is what I remember.

I remember my father's broken English and heavy Greek accent. I recall how he treated my mother with such gentleness and genuine love. I remember everyday my father bringing me something. Sometimes it was a piece of candy. Sometimes it was a shiny penny. And sometimes it was a toy. But all the time it was love. I used to get so excited to hear him coming up the stairs of the apartment building. I jumped and bounced for joy when I heard the key enter the lock and saw the doorknob turning. He used to lift me high, swirl around, and dance with me. Those were the golden days.

He was proud of his Greek heritage but embraced being an American. He was Greek Orthodox and practiced that religion but never forced it upon mother or me. He always made me speak English and didn't want me to learn Greek. He said I was an American with Greek heritage and I had to honor both, but above all things, I was an American. Oh, to hear his voice once again and to see his eyes dance when he first saw me. I felt love. I knew love.

It all came crashing down one day after my sixth birthday. I was playing in the back portion of the restaurant. My uncle Tom was cooking at the grill and my father was playing cards. I heard shouting, shots rang out, and when I looked up to see what was going on, I saw my father plummet to the floor. Uncle Tom ran to me and covered me with his body. I think he was shot as well.

That night, we were taken away to Pine Haven Lodge and stayed with 'Uncle' Pug and 'Aunt' Mabel. I asked what happened and where was my daddy, but mother refused to talk about it. She took that terrible night and all its secrets with her to her grave. I found myself alone without the guiding light of a father. Smitty tried to help me as did 'Uncle' Pug, but it wasn't the same. They treated me well, but I wanted my daddy.

It took a while, but I finally settled in and made friends. I actually love it there and to this day I consider Pine Haven (Now Pine Ridge) my home. The days in that little two room log cabin are priceless. At the age of twelve I discovered that nothing last forever.

We left Red Oak, Michigan for what I thought was a visit to my uncles. I didn't pack any of my toys. I didn't say goodbye to my dog Frosty that I so loved. I left my beautiful green Schwinn bike by the old horse hitching post. I didn't get to say goodbye to my beloved classmates. But most of all, I didn't think that this would be the last time I ever would see my aunt, uncle, and Smitty. If I could only have closer for those moments…

We moved and once again mother never shared with me why. I begged her to go back but she wouldn't even talk about it. My heart once again ached, and my thoughts were of my father. Why wasn't he there to protect me and guide my footsteps. The pains of feeling abandoned permeated my heart. I found myself living with three bachelor uncles and my mother in a one-bedroom house. The dining area was converted into a bedroom, but it had no privacy. Everyone had to walk through there to get to the kitchen and the living room door was nonexistent. Soon, I found myself existing and not living as I dreamed. I wanted my daddy and when I went to the outhouse at night, I would cry and ask God to give him back to me.

Another man entered our lives and my world crumbled. We moved into an old shack and soon I realized this man drank, cursed and was an abuser. I hated being there. I began changing. I had no guidance or father figure. I was simply tolerated. I began to drift and run with the wrong crowd. I was a manipulator and could change colors like a chameleon. For years I was lost and felt so all alone.

I married after the army and had two beautiful children. I loved them with all my heart, but I had no idea on how to be a father or husband. All I had seen was dysfunction and abuse. I found myself depressed, alone and once again, I felt abandoned. Why didn't I have a father figure to guide me? After a long struggle, I realized I no skills, no experiences, no guidance to be a father. I made the hardest decision of my life and to this day I am haunted by it. I realized the marriage was gone and staying would damage my beloved little ones. For their sake I away not realizing that I could have learned how to be a father.

Today I still am burdened by leaving and pay the price for not being there for them. Rarely do I see them and then, only in passing. I have missed the most important thing in life: family.

Then I met a man who has never forsaken me. Then I met a fisher of men who so loved me that he clung to a cross for six hours before crying out, "It is finished"! Then I found a father figure who was there all along. He never left me. He never abandoned me. I had abandoned him.

I found what I had missed all my life! I found the perfect father! I found unconditional love and someone who genuinely loved me. He said He would not leave me as an orphan; He would come to me (John 14:18). He kept his promise.

Though I still don't see my grown children any and wouldn't know my grandbabies if they came up to me, this I know. The man that I was has gone. I am a new creator in Christ. Old things have been put aside. All things are now new. Even in the darkest of night, He is with me. He comforts me in the valley of the shadow of death. I fear no evil. I have finally realized I had a father all along and maybe by His grace, he will once again give me a chance to become the father, the daddy that I was destined to be.

I thank God for those times I felt abandoned for I can tell other; I was not alone. I thank God for my poor abilities in being a daddy, for I can counsel others and by example help them heal the hurts and become the fathers they were destined to be. I thank God that in spite of my failures my children have become fine outstanding Christians. I didn't give them the roots they needed but I am so thankful they have the wings that are strong.

Maybe before I cross that turbid veil, I will be given another chance to show my grow children that I have become the father that I longed to have so many years ago.

My prayer is this: *"My Dear God, thank you for your protection and giving me a spiritual family. If it be your will, I beseech thee to give me another chance at being a father who walks in your footsteps."*

PRAYER TREES

"Again Jesus began to teach by the lake. The crowd that gathered around him was so large that he got into a boat and sat in it out on the lake, while all the people were along the shore at the water's edge. He taught them many things by parables, and in his teaching said: "Listen! A farmer went out to sow his seed. As he was scattering the seed, some fell along the path, and the birds came and ate it up. Some fell on rocky places, where it did not have much soil. It sprang up quickly, because the soil was shallow. But when the sun came up, the plants were scorched, and they withered because they had no root. Other seed fell among thorns, which grew up and choked the plants, so that they did not bear grain. Still other seed fell on good soil. It came up, grew and produced a crop, some multiplying thirty, some sixty, some a hundred times." Mark 4:1-8

Years ago, when hearts were young, and innocence was in full bloom, I used to take my Tonya and David to the waterfalls above the old house. The waterfalls is about twelve feet high and the water cascades from, what was known as the Water Rocks, plummeted into a small pool. There was a small branch flowing on the right side of the hollow and a small peninsula had been created over time.

I recall our first excursion to the falls. It was cold, and the little branch had frozen over with a thick layer of ice. We bundled up and walked up the branch on the ice. Their little eyes danced with excitement and discovery. I am sure there was a little fear as well, but they had full confidence in the daddy.

As we approached the falls, they heard the sound of water falling off the cliff into the pool. They got so excited! We walked to where the big rocks on the left side of the cliff conceal the falls and then, eureka, there it was in all its splendor! I can still hear my daughter exclaim how beautiful it was and my son wanting to skate on the ice formed in the pool.

As we walked on the peninsula, they noted a small pine tree growing. One of them said it would be a good Christmas tree. Considering the season, I thought so as well, but we already had a tree in the house. I suggested getting a couple of ornaments and bringing them back to decorate the little scrub pine. They were in total agreement!

After spending time around the falls, me sharing a few stories of my youth, and how importance the falls was to me. You see, in summer the falls was my shower. It was my swimming hole though only waist deep. And when troubled or fearful, the falls was my refuge. To see them excited about the falls made me realize how fortunate I was to have them in close proximity to my old shack.

We went back and talked about decorating the tree. Finally, we decided to only take a couple and each year to take one decoration up and place it on the little pine. We walked back with our treasures and as I watched them place their offerings to the tree, I could not contain my joy. Tears came into my eyes and when Tonya saw my emotion, she got worried. She asked what was wrong. I grabbed both of their glove covered hands and said, "Nothing is wrong, in fact, EVERYTHING is right." We called the little sapling the Jesus Tree and offered a short prayer.

Each year we offered a decoration to that tree. As it grew, I went up and ensured the decorations were not too tight on the growing limbs. I remember that I got so used to praying when I saw the tree that I decided to plant other bushes in honor of those precious moments we had when Camelot was in full bloom.

The tradition faded but on occasion, we did follow the ritual. Then came the time when they grew up, went to college, and formed their own lives. I found myself walking to the falls in deep thought. How I missed those days and wanted them to know that though they were gone, I still walked with them in my heart.

Then an idea hit me. I decoded that I would place rocks along the banks of that little brook. I decided to just put place a couple every time I walked to the falls. Soon the path was lined with rocks. Another idea came regarding a rock wall connected to the big rock that I used as a step to walk on the bridge (another idea). It was built a stone at a time.

Then I decided I needed a bench. After rebuilding an old bench, I wanted to have a swing so when I went I could enjoy the rocking as I listened to the sounds of God's wonders. I added a small fire pit for those cold days and/or nights when I needed to meditate, pray, and seek guidance when troubled.

The greatest idea came to me as I decorated the Jesus Tree one Christmas. I hadn't seen the kids and was finding myself becoming depressed. Instead of being upset or feeling sorry for myself, I walked to the falls that night. The stars seemed to be shining just for me and the fire I had build offered a glow that mesmerized me. I heard an owl and he seemed to call my name. I had nowhere to go but to my knees. As I prayed for forgiveness and safety for my grown children, something inside me stirred. Suddenly, my mind came up with an idea of planting Prayer Trees for the sick, infirmed and to honor those that had passed through the turbid veil.

I was elated, but I realized I had to wait until it was time to plant trees. As I thought about it, I decided I would plant one tree for each person that was in my heart. I came up with a ritual of when I planted a tree, I would 'Christian' it with a name for the person in my prayers. Each tree, each scrub, each plant, and each stone represented someone and on occasion, something.

I plan to continue doing but I also wish for others to follow the concept. One of my dearest friends passed away and we planted a tree in his memory. The family told me that somehow that act of planting a tree had brought them comfort. I think it involves faith, hope, and love, for these are the ingredients of unconditional and everlasting love. As the tree grows so does the memory. The prayer tree stretches to heaven and God listens to the prayers of the people.

Friend, you are welcome to join me, as I create Pine Haven Falls, a place where serenity and sacredness dwells. It is a place where hope, peace, and love abound. Bring an evergreen (holly, mountain laurel, pine tree, shrub) and plant it with a prayer for someone. The soil is good, and the harvest will be great.

ARE YOU DOCTOR SEUSS?

"If there be therefore any consolation in Christ, if any comfort of love, if any fellowship of the Spirit, if any bowels and mercies, fulfill ye my joy, that ye be likeminded, having the same love, being of one accord, of one mind. Let nothing be done through strife or vainglory; but in lowliness of mind let each esteem other better than themselves. Look not every man on his own things, but every man also on the things of others. " Philippians 1: 1-4

Today I had the honor to speak to some delightful children. I dressed up in my persona and practiced what I was going to say. I just knew I was going to razzle dazzle those little five through ten-year-old children. After all, I had been doing this for several years and knew my material. My confidence level was high, and I fear, so was my prideful spirit.

I walked into the library and there running around the room were the images of innocence. I met with the supervisor and then, out of the corner of my eye, I noted they saw me in all my regalia. I was in for a warm reception. They pointed and stared not knowing what character stepped out of the history book, but I was sure I was going to educate them on my persona.

One beautiful little six-year-old girl spotted me and came running over to me. I knew in my heart that she recognized my character. I smiled to myself and greeted her with grand anticipation of being recognized. That darling little cherub looked me square in the eyes and said, *"Are you Doctor Seuss?"*

My ego ruptured with embarrassment, as it was deflated like a tire running over spikes! That precious child had brought me back to the world of reality and I realized that I had not entered this venue with humility of spirit nor had I asked God to give me the words. Needless to say, my performance was mediocre at best, but I still received numerous hugs for my effort.

Friend, have you ever allowed your ego, foolish pride, and stubbornness get in the way of your mission in life? I have on many occasions. The Bible tells us in Proverbs 11:2, *"When pride comes, then comes disgrace, but with humility comes wisdom."* Lesson Learned!

God does not disregard a haughty spirt. He will not tolerate arrogance. He wants us to humble ourselves and help others without thought of reward for ourselves. The Bible has many verses pertaining to such self-inflation. Read the words of our God in Luke 18: 10-14. *"Two men went up into the temple to pray: the one a Pharisee, and the other a publican. The Pharisee stood and prayed thus with himself, God, I thank thee, that I am not as other men are, extortioners, unjust, adulterers, or even as this publican. I fast twice in the week, I give tithes of all that I possess. And the publican, standing afar off, would not lift up so much as his eyes unto heaven, but smote upon his breast, saying, God be merciful to me a sinner. I tell you, this man went down to his house justified rather than the other: for every one that exalteth himself shall be abased; and he that humbleth himself shall be exalted."*

Friend let us humble ourselves before the Lord often. Let us pray for forgiveness and resist the temptations of the devil's lair. James 4:10 shows us the way. He says that God will exalt you if you humble yourselves before Him. By definition, the word exalt means to glorify, to praise, to raise up and elevate. Wouldn't you rather be praised by our God than by man? That is a no brainer.

So, with humble gratitude I say to the little cherub, "No dear child, I am not Doctor Seuss, but only a man humbled by your innocence."

THE BEAM THAT BLINDS

"Judge not that ye be not judged. For with what judgment ye judge, ye shall be judged: and with what measure ye mete, it shall be measured to you again. And why beholds thou the mote that is in thy brother's eye, but considerest not the beam that is in thine own eye" Matthew 7:1-3

The other day I happen to encounter an old high school friend. He looked the same and had the same voice, but he was different. I knew he was a regular at his church and practiced his faith. I was in for a shock.

We started talking about some old classmates and I mentioned one in particular. I told my old friend that everywhere our former classmate went, he listened to Bible tapes. I also mentioned that he could quote scripture to fit the occasion. My old friend interrupted me and said, *"Listening to the tapes and quoting scripture won't get you into heaven. Only accepting the Lord Jesus Christ as your personal savior will."* He had missed the point and I was a tad taken back by his pompousness and know it all attitude.

Don't get me wrong, I know he is a godly man and has done great works for Christ. Oh, I admit he was right in stating that Christ is the one and only way to eternal life. BUT who are we to judge another person? I do not know the condition of my other friend's soul. I do know that once when he was very sick with cancer that he told me he was ready to meet his maker but didn't want to buck the line! I too can identify with that statement! I also realize that God gave us free will and the choice we make is a personal one. Our job is to lead the sheep to the Living Water. A friend once said that all we do is catch the fish and the Great Fisherman CLEANS the fish!

Friend, the problem today is that we tend to judge prior to speaking. We preach to the choir, shake hands with our brothers and sisters, pat 'our church members' on the back, yet sometimes we forget our Great Commission. I am reminded of Jesus's words in Matthew 23:1-37. Christ is very blunt in His disgust for those men and women who are hypocritical. He talks of the leaders of the church and how they do works to be seen by men and love the best places in the seats of the churches. They wish to be called by manmade sanctified names. They beat upon their chests like the great beasts and proclaim all they have done. Yet they neglect the widow. Yet they forget that we are to humble ourselves and seek out those lost sheep.

Christ walked amongst those that others looked down up and even judged our savior by their hypocritic standards. Listen to the words of our God in verse 37, as he laments Jerusalem. *"O*

Jerusalem, Jerusalem, the one who kills the prophets and stones those who are sent to her! How often I wanted to gather your children together, as a hen gathers her chicks under her wings, but you were not willing! [38] See! Your house is left to you desolate; [39] for I say to you, you shall see Me no more till you say, 'Blessed is He who comes in the name of the LORD!'"

Friend make no mistake; I too have been like the Pharisees of olden times. I have thumped my chest and proclaimed my good works but came to realize that all is vain unless the spirit of the Lord is within me and I go in His name, humbly helping others to realize their morning song, without thought of reward for myself. We all must remove the beam from our eye and go forward serving others and bringing the lost to our Shepherd.

BEARING OUR BURDENS

"Bear ye one another's burdens, and so fulfil the law of Christ. For if a man think himself to be something, when he is nothing, he deceiveth himself. But let every man prove his own work, and then shall he have rejoicing in himself alone, and not in another. For every man shall bear his own burden. Let him that is taught in the word communicate unto him that teacheth in all good things. Be not deceived; God is not mocked: for whatsoever a man soweth, that shall he also reap. For he that soweth to his flesh shall of the flesh reap corruption; but he that soweth to the Spirit shall of the Spirit reap life everlasting."
Galatians 2-8

The other day I was talking to a friend and she shared what I consider a very valid statement. She said that reputation is what others say about you, but character is what you do. I recall reading that character is what you do when no one is watching. Both are truths. The definition of character includes the words trait, moral, ethics, uniqueness, and the arrogate of features that form the individual nature of someone. All are good definitions but pale in comparison to God's defining statements.

The Bible tells us that each person 'must prove his own work' and that what is sown shall be reaped.

Harsh? No, not at all. God wants us to follow His Son's footsteps as best as humanly possible. We will never be perfect and there will be those moments, those days, and those times that the devil will test us. It is then that our Christian character must shine through and resist the creature from the depths. The Bible tells us that if we resist the devil he will flee from us. Another great truth is that God is greater and more powerful. He has power over the demons and He will not leave us as orphans.

Friends we must sow in the spirit and think of helping others help themselves. We are to fulfill the law of Christ and assist in carrying the burdens of our brothers and sisters. AND we must do so with humility. It has been said that we must do unto others and have no thought of reward for ourselves.

One of my friends gives items to the needy on several occasions and asks that no one knows of the benefactor. He and his wife read the paper, work through helping and healing agencies to find a needy family or person. Then they help with the NEED, not the want. This is an act of sowing.

Friend the need is great and the sowers are few. Let us all remember the cause of Christ and how we can show character as do angels unaware. Bear our burdens and those of others and follow Him.

WHEN IN DOUBT

"Is any sick among you? Let him call for the elders of the church, and let them pray over him, anointing him with oil in the name of the Lord, and the prayer of faith will save the one who is sick, and the Lord will rise him up. And if he has committed sins, he will be forgiven. Therefore confess your sins to one another and pray for one another, that you may be healed. The prayer of a righteous person has great power as it is working."
James 5:14-16

Mother always told me, *"Son, when in doubt, pray."* It took a while for me to fully grasp the significance of her statement. God is only a fervent prayer away. He is not the God of afar but the God of closeness. He is all around you. You can see Him in the forest, in the meadow, among the flowers, in the sky and on the mountains. You can hear His voice on the wind, in the babbling water and the sounds in the woodland. His touch is upon the wind and the breeze that refreshes. You can taste His nectar in the water and the food you eat. He is also within us. He is omnipotent.

The power of prayer is amazing. Christ stated for us to only ask and it would be given unto us! We are to seek, and we shall find. Simply knock and the door will be open! Read Matthew 7:7 and believe. Then look at Mark 11:24 and you will discover the same thing! He is our amazing Savior!

Prayer is not a monolog but rather a dialogue. John Bunyan said that, *"Prayer is a shield to the soul, a sacrifice to God and a scourge to satan."* How very true! The demons tremble when we pray. They seek dark corners and hide in fear. Greater is He that is in me than he that is in the world!

Dear friends do not be anxious for anything. Philippians 4:6-7 tells us the good news of the gospel. Let us therefore step out in faith, rejoicing in our supplications, and embracing the peace that passes all understanding. For this day, I live with the knowledge that prayers change things. My heart is guarded if it is guided by earnest prayer. Thank you, mother, for those five simple, yet most powerful words, *"Son, when in doubt pray."*

(Hour of Decision by Marie Merritt)

GOD'S MYSTERIOUS WAYS

"As thou knowest not what is the way of the spirit, nor how the bones do grow in the womb of her that is with child: even so thou knowest not the works of God who maketh all."
Ecclesiastes 11:5

In 1773, William Cowper wrote a poem/song entitled, 'God Moves in Mysterious Ways'. The manner in which he wrote the song is a grand example of God's mystery. This is his story.

William was born in 1731, at Berkhamsted, England. When he was six years old, his mother died leaving him under the care of his father. Their relationship was rocky and soon William exhibited signs of depression. His condition worsened to the point of attempting suicide on many occasions. He was institutionalized in an insane asylum. But God works in mysterious ways.

In 1764, at the age of 33, he was saved. Three years later he became friends with another man touched by the mysterious ways of God. His name was John Newton. Together they compiled a book of hymns. The famed write of Amazing Grace contributed 208 hymns to the book and William Cowper wrote 68! For the remainder of his life, William followed Christ and believed in his wisdom, power, and goodness. He found salvation from depression, suicide, and anxiety through the mysterious ways of God!

It still rings true today. I have personally experienced His mysterious ways numerous times in my life. It continues to this day.

A couple of weeks ago I received a message from an Emilie B. who lived in Michigan. She had been to an estate or vendor's mall and found a letter, along with post cards from a World War I soldier. She looked online (I imagine by typing in the name of Private Preston Dickenson) and noted that I had compiled a book about the Dickenson boys from letters found at an estate sale in northern Michigan. The name of the book is, Lost Letters From a Dough Boy.

We began corresponding and she offered to send me the letters and postcards! I was overjoyed. The letter was dated October 7, 1918. One of the postcards was dated July 22, 1915. Upon receiving the historical gifts, I nervously opened the envelope. Within the confines of the letter, I once again found a family legacy filled with love and devotion. I immediately began typing the letter, scanned the postcards and included them in the book for the 2nd edition publication! The same feeling of having Preston and his brother, Clinton, sitting beside me as I recorded his words overwhelmed me. I savored every word. God's handiwork was obvious!

The manner in which I was given the other letters and postcards in 2015, which later became the book, is yet another example of God working in mysterious ways. The following was taken from the FOREWORD of <u>Lost Letters From a Dough Boy</u>.

"Rarely in life does a writer encounter a wondrous opportunity not only to share a story but also to preserve history. My opportunity knocked unexpectedly. It was as if the moon and stars aligned themselves and offered me chance to gaze into the past while preserving it for the future.

"I had traveled to Mio, Michigan, and was visiting some of the places of my youth. I decided to drive to Lewiston and visit the lakes I used to frequent as a young lad. At the four-way stop I noted a little antique shop (Antique Depot) and decided to browse. I was greeted by a lady from Mississippi and talked to her for a few moments. The owner of the store came in and she too was very friendly. She introduced herself as Debbie. We began talking and I discovered she had a son by the name of Matthew who had served in Iraq and had been wounded. I offered my book entitled <u>Unsung Heroes</u> and gave her my card.

"The next day I received a phone call from her and asked me to come to her shop to meet Matthew and that they had something for me. I agreed and drove from the Gaylord area (I had been to St. Ignace) back to Lewiston. It was a quiet Sunday afternoon when I arrived.

Debbie immediately called her son and I was soon honored to meet the fine young man. Then I was presented with a large bag of letters from a dough boy. I was overwhelmed when I realized that in my possession was the story of not only one soldier but two and the communique between family members during World War One. I could not thank my new-found friends enough for their generosity.

"That evening as I sat in the motel, I read my first letter from a dough boy. Within the confines of the letter was another piece of American history that had been lost for almost one hundred years. I was hooked. I was intrigued. In my possession I held letters from young men who lived in a small area in West Virginia, known as Brandywine. How did these forgotten letters end up several hundred miles in northern Michigan? Whatever happened to Privates Clinton and Preston Dickenson? Where are the descendants and are they aware of having World War I heroes in their ancestry?

"I asked God for guidance. Therein I began my quest for answers and an endeavor to weave a

tapestry of not only the Dickenson family but also insight into the lives of people who lived in that almost forgotten bygone era. The search continues but I pray that the letters, pictures, and other pertinent information will someday link the broken circle and paint the picture of those forgotten heroes of World War One."

Friend, God's goodness is all around us. Friend, God's mysterious ways surround us. Friend, His ways are mighty, pure and in our best interest. Friend, this day allow him to enter and find the sweet surrender, along with the serenity of a peace that passes all understanding. Bathe in the light of God's mysterious ways.

"For my thoughts are not your thoughts, neither are your ways my ways," declares the Lord." As the heavens are higher than the earth, so are my ways higher than your ways and my thoughts than your thoughts."
Isaiah 55: 8-9

Resource

https://www.challies.com/articles/hymn-stories-god-moves-in-a-mysterious-way/

TO RISE ABOVE THE STORM

*"Whoever dwells in the shelter of the Most High
will rest in the shadow of the Almighty."*
Psalm 91:1

Friends, I have pondered and prayed about writing
on this subject. It seems that God has led me to do
so. I am referring to the storm we are currently
attempting to withstand without God's protection.

It is all around me. I see it wherever I go. I was
getting gas the other day and noted two men
fighting right in front of the pumps. One had the
other in a choke hold and hitting him unmercifully
in the back of the head. An older lady was cursing
at the top of her lungs at the one hitting the other. I
had to intervene. My reward was to be cursed out
by both parties. What did they learn? Old men can
be dangerous when backed into a corner! The
reason for the fight? The one being choked owed
the other one money. For what, you ask? Need I
say it: drugs! There is an epidemic in our area, in
our county, in our state, and within our nation.

Hepatitis A is rampant in our area. In fact, a recent
study showed we lead the nation in Hepatitis A
and Hepatitis C is sweeping the nation. The
reason? Drugs and needles. Ask anyone around in
our section of the country about finding needles.
They are becoming as common as trash along the

highway. They are lying along the roads. They are hidden in the weeds. They have been found on playgrounds and ball fields. In fact, one parent told me he found five needles near the dugout where his grandchildren practice little league ball! Unintentionally, the distribution of free needles through the needle exchange program has only escalated the problem. The person using will inject him or herself, then discard the needle 'helter skelter'. They also continue to share needles with another. The program of offering free needles is liken unto a codependent enabling the spouse. The answer isn't free needles but rather freedom through Christ! Satan offers the syringe, but Christ offers salvation!

Christ was removed from our schools. How is that working for you, America? Christ is being pushed on of our homes and replaced by apathy, disrespect, disregard, and discontentment abounds. Remember that the, 'Discontented child cries for toasted snow'. We see self-centered mannerisms, put downs, bullying and hatred. Take a look at 'comedy' on TV. The vulgar and downright nasty put downs by so called comedians is sickening. We have placed TV and sports personalities above our own ability to make judgement calls. After all, they are successful, so they must be knowledgeable about everything. They poison our minds and souls with their pervasive nature we allow into our homes nightly. There is a lack of manners, courtesy, and morals. We have plummeted from the teaching of our true God and allowed others dictate our thinking. And let us not forget about this thing called, 'political correctness'! Where did this term originate and what does it mean? Personally, I would much rather be morally right than politically correct.

America, no is not a bad word! Standing tall for God and His values is our responsibility, nay, our duty as Christians. You will either have the pain of discipline now or the morbid pain of regret later. There is a storm cloud over our country. Let us rise above the storm.

How can we fight this appalling tornado sweeping over our nation? The answer is simple; it can be found in the Bible. Let us look at the founding fathers and their desire to have Christian education and Christian homes as the foundation of our country. Let us stand and simply say enough, while we reinstitute reading the Bible in the evening as a family. Salvation restores sanity! Require your children to be able to recite verses from God's word. Remember your parents praying before eating? Remember praying before you went to bed? Remember going to church and not being asked to if you wanted to go but rather you're going and be ready in fifteen minutes? Are you ready meant we are leaving shortly, so don't make me come in there!

Turn off the TV and monitor what they watch where their eyes go on the internet and who talk to them when they are on these modern-day devices. Be the example your family, your children, your friends so desperately need. America, fall down upon your knees and ask for a healing of our nation! Let us turn from our wicked ways and seek refuge within the confines of God's arms. Let us all stand tall and rise above the storm.

"If my people, who are called by my name, shall humble themselves, and pray, and seek my face, and turn from their wicked ways; then will I hear from heaven, and will forgive their sin, and will heal their land." 2 Corinthians 7:14

A PONY WITH PAINTED 'TOENAILS'

*"Children are a heritage from the Lord, offspring
a reward from him."*
Psalm 127:3

I was in a vendor's mall browsing as is my custom, when suddenly an object caught my eye. There on the floor was a fairly large plastic pony with red 'toenails'! I had to laugh, as a flood of memories flowed of a time of innocence and the joy of witnessing my children grow. It reminded me how lucky I was to have been a witness to such imaging of a child.

Years ago, my daughter wanted a play pony. I searched for the longest time and finally found a rather large brown pony with a mane and tail she could comb. That was one of her requests. I was rather proud of the find but wanted to surprise her. I placed it behind a chair in the living room and didn't say a word to anyone about it.

My son was the first to discover it. I had him give an oath of silence regarding not telling his sister. He kept his word after a little bribe. I had bought him a toy that he wanted in exchange for his silence!

I couldn't help but notice that when my daughter saw her brother playing with a new action figure, she looked sort of puzzled, as if to say, "Daddy, where's my surprise?".

I saw that look in her eyes and couldn't contain myself any longer. I asked her if she would get something I said I dropped and rolled behind the chair. Being such an obedient child, she immediately complied to my request. When she turned the corner and saw the pony, she squealed with delight. Then came the tears of joy. and that magical hug I still long for. She was one happy little lady!

We started playing together, my son with his action figure and my daughter with her play pony. We enjoyed the imaging for a while. Then daughter came up with the idea of having a tea party and invited my son, his newest toy, and of course, her pony. She declared it to be a formal affair and asked that we dress accordingly.

My son put all the accessories on his action figure. Much to his displeasure, I combed his hair and washed off his face and hands. I put on a nice shirt over top of my old worn-out T-shirt. My daughter seemed to be thinking. Then she asked me how she could dress up her pony. She didn't have a saddle or bridle but wanted the pony to be dressed up. I suggested that we put make-up on the pony. She didn't seem to like that suggestion too much. Suddenly she said, "I know, we can paint its toes!" I tried to keep from laughing and gave her the OK wink that was a custom between me and the kids.

She borrowed some nail polish from a drawer belonging to her mother and we sat in the floor painting the hoofs a bright red! She worked tirelessly and soon the project was finished. She combed the play pony's mane and tail. Then she put two little red bows on it. One went on it mane and the other on its tail. The pony was ready for the social event of the day. She was so proud of her play pony.

We sat around the tea set laid out in perfection upon the floor and began chatting. She opened up with a childhood pray and of course, manners were observed when accepting the 'tea' and 'cookies'. My son fed his newfound friend and my daughter insured that her guest was well fed. My soul was lifted to heights beyond my imagination watching the scene unfold. That moment became one of many precious memoires.

I am not sure what happened to the action figure or the play pony. Yet before me was an opportunity to relive those moments with my children. I didn't care about the price of the pony with red toenails, I only knew I had to have it. I took it to the counter and purchased it; all the while trying not to cry. I was not successful in that endeavor.

And now the little play pony has a place of honor in my house. It is surrounded by pictures of horses and figures to remind me of true love passed on during a magic moment while sitting on a floor with two cherubs, an action figure, and a play pony with red toenails.

"Only take care, and keep your soul diligently, lest you forget the things that your eyes have seen, and lest they depart from your heart all the days of your life. Make them known to your children and your children's children."
Deuteronomy 4:9

Jesus said, "Let the little children come to me, and do not hinder them, for the kingdom of heaven belongs to such as these." *15 When he had placed his hands on them, he went on from there.*
Matthew 19:14

THE HITCH HIKER

"Therefore Go and make disciples of all nations, baptizing them in the name of the Father and the Son and of the Holy Spirit, and teaching them to obey everything I have commanded you. And surely I am with you always, to the very end of the age." Matthew 28:19-20

Everyone knew him. He was always walking along the road with a red bandana tied to his forehead. He usually wore a bright red or orange t-shirt with the number 7 on it. He carried a backpack and thumbed wherever he went.

I recalled picking him up on occasion and speaking to him just to make conversation. He spoke with a lisp and was hard to understand. I never really got to know him all that well.

I was eating lunch at a local diner I noted him walking towards me. He had a big grin on his face and was talking a mile a minute. He thanked me for my kindness and gave me a plastic bag with something in it. I thanked him, and he left. After I ate, I went to the car and looked inside the bag. I was surprised by his gift. It was a 3x5 Christian flag. Not once had I asked him about his soul's condition. Not once had I asked him to attend church with me. Not once had I asked him to break bread. Yet there in my hand was a gift from a man I really didn't know that well. I realized I had failed my commission.

The next day I went looking for him. I went to all the places I knew he frequented and asked the clerks had they seen him. Not one person recalled seeing him that day. I thought that was very strange. I decided to drive along the road where he was always seen thumbing a ride.

I drove about fifteen miles and just before the three-way traffic light, there were several cars backed up along the highway. I became curious and so I got out of my car and walked to where several men were standing talking and looking into the horizon. I walked up to the men and was greeted by them. I asked what the delay was. They said they didn't know but apparently there had been an accident.

I walked back to my car and sat down for what seemed to be the longest time. I found myself getting impatient and frustrated. I wanted to find that man who had given me the flag and invite him to church. Besides, I didn't have the time to waste.

In about forty minutes the line of cars began slowly moving. I started my car and inched my way up. After a mile or so I came upon the scene of the accident. The ambulance had gone but the car was still there along with several police officers. I glanced in that direction and to my horror, I noted a red bandana and a backpack lying beside the curb. I stopped and asked the officer what happened. He stated that a man had been hit. I asked was he alright and the officer didn't answer. He simply waved me on so other cars could get past the scene of the accident.

I turned around and went home praying that he had not been killed. I turned on the local news and listened to the report. The newscast stated there had been an accident but did not release the name of the victim. When I heard the word victim, I knew someone had died. I prayed earnestly for that person, hoping it wasn't my hitchhiking friend.

The news came around eleven that night. The name of the victim was released and to my dismay, it was the man so many knew as only the hitch hiker. My heart sank because I did not ask him about his relationship with Christ. I had the opportunity but failed in keeping my commission as a Christian.

The reporter continued talking and stated that upon examining the backpack, the police had found seventeen Christian flags in it. Several people were interviewed stating that he had given them a flag for their kindness.

Suddenly it donned upon me that I need not ask about his soul's condition. His works showed that he indeed following the cross. I cried for him and for my lack of concern. I fell on my knees and made a promise that I would never allow an opportunity to pass me by again to share the Great Commission with another.

WHEN INNOCENSE RODE THE WIND

*"A man that hath friends must shew himself
friendly: and there is a friend that sticketh closer
than a brother."*
Proverbs 18:24

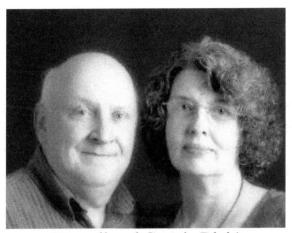

(Russell and Connie Blair)

I thought it would never end. We were to live forever: all the while running the hills of ageless innocence. But the walls of Camelot came tumbling down with his passing.

I recall so many vivid memories. I was the Cisco Kid and he was Poncho. In reality, it should have been the other way around. I was the Lone Ranger and he was Tonto. He should have been the Ranger and I HIS sidekick. So many precious memoires.

One of my favorite images captured in my mind is of Arlin James, Deanna, Russell, and Janet wearing cowboy/cowgirl outfits when we lived in Michigan. I can still hear the sounds of the gunfights, horse hooves beating the sod, and the cry of 'Hi Oh Silver Away' meandering within the apartment walls!

I recall Aunt Gay visiting us at Pine Haven Lodge in Red Oak, Michigan, and the pure joy of 'performing' for her and mother while they watched me play near the hitching posts placed in the yard. I would yell out for my 'pards' Arlin and Russ, to come to my aid as I held off the bandits until they arrived.

I remember moving to Perkins Branch and the feeling of loneliness and separation from my friends that I left behind at Red Oak School. I was frightened on the first day of school. During recess I recall a boy in my class looking and pointing at me. He was laughing and then came over and said, "Hi you guys". Then I realized that I was alone and wasn't accepted. I was made fun of by a bully for having an accent. To this day he belittles others to make himself appear better than them. All that changed when my cousins came. No one dared make fun of us and before long, I was accepted.

So many memories are flooding my mind. They come in flashes, as if lightning. I recall all the times we hung out at the head of Perkins Branch where my Uncle Ess and Aunt Myrtle lived. It was the old family place. Uncle Arlie (Jack) and Aunt Gay had lived below the last house in the holler (Uncle Elsie's farm) and that is where Arlin, Deanna, and Russ lived. Can't recall if Janet was born then. The house burnt many years ago. Uncle Arlie was in the army (served in Korea where he was severely wounded).

We used to play above Uncle Ess's house at the old coal bank. We climbed every rock up there and was oblivious to snakes or other creatures that lived in and around such structures. Then there were the times we walked up to the head of the holler eating mulberries and other eatable plants along the way. We would splash through the branch and throw rocks at anything that dared move, including each other. We had tarpon races and played in the old barn.

Then there were the times we stayed with Uncle Charlie, Uncle Granville, and Uncle Dennis. We played all up and down the hog pen and made our way to the creek by wading the branch to the mouth of the holler. We would run along the path to the swinging bridge close to Granville and Dennis's store just off highway seven. In those days, the car road ran through the creek and there was nothing but that old swinging bride, a path around the point and a small foot bridge near the back of Josie Hampton's barn to get up and down the holler. In fact, we had to ford the branch several times to get to the head of the left or right-hand fork of the holler.

I can't count the number of times I walked from my house to their house just to play. I usually crossed the railroad bridge. It was dangerous to do so but I liked stepping on the ties and the smell of creosote. There was a swinging bridge just above the railroad, but I rather cross the railroad. We used to fish and swim below the swinging bridge. It wasn't a deep hole but fun.

I remember when floods came, I would go to their house and we would try to bust the bottles floating down the swollen creek. We saw no danger and really knew no fear. In our youth we felt the flames of invincibility.

My mind wondered to the time that we bought that old farm off Uncle Arlie and Aunt Gay. We paid $600 for it in installments. Fifty dollars a month came out of my Social Security check until it was paid in full. I think we bought it in the mid-fifties. Later I remember Uncle Arlie staying with us for several weeks and how I enjoyed listening to his tales.

There was one time when I was a senior that Russell got stung in the face and his eyes swelled shut. Someone started calling him Hop Sing, which was a name he didn't like. Hop Sing was a character on Bonanza. One morning we were in the hall at school and the bully you used to make fun of me saw Russ coming and called him that name. Everyone around the bully laughed but me. I shoved him against the locker and we began fighting. I was determined to break his head, but a teacher broke us up before I could do much damage. It was one thing to joke with someone but never is it alright to make fun and belittle. I couldn't and still won't stand for such. I don't think I ever shared that with Russ or Arlin. I know what Arlin would have done to protect his little brother.

I still hear his laugh and his keen wit. The only laugh to drown him out would be Deanna, his sister. She could make me laugh anytime and I loved her so for the way she tried to protect my mother. Again, in those days we took care of our own.

Russ was so intelligent. Arlin, Russ, and I went into a business adventure together. For the life of me, all I can remember is the good times and the laughter. I do recall me being a jerk on occasion! When Russ went to the army, his skills were quickly recognized, he was placed in a special unit in Vietnam. I will leave it at that. Once he was discharged he studied and became a United States Marshall. I think he was the only one in our family to ever achieve such an honor. After Arlin's service in Vietnam, he became a police officer as well. The key word in their family was service to the people.

I don't believe Russ ever lost some of that childhood innocence and I can honestly state for a fact that he was genuine in his love for his family and his wife of fifty years. He was humble in spirit, quick witted and above all, one of the most forgiving individuals I have ever known. I wish I could gain that characteristic at the level he possessed.

I remember in 1989 when Russ was involved in a terrible accident. In fact, we thought we had lost him. But he survived. His still mouth was wired together, and he shared a story with me about an incident that occurred. He was driving, and a vehicle passed him in an unsafe manner. Russ hit the blue lights and pulled the man over. Russ said he was very mad and was giving the driver the riot act. Abruptly, he realized that the poor driver had no idea of what he was saying because his mouth was wired so tight that Russ was hard to understand! I can still see that in my mind's eye and smile every time I think of that incident.

Another memory was of Jean's restaurant. Aunt Gay (and later my mother) worked there. It became our 'hanging out' place. We'd meet there and go to the creek to skip rocks, talk of things to come. I don't know why but I happened to remember the Archie Comic books. I acted like I didn't like girls and Russ called me Jughead, after one of the characters. I liked that character and so I started calling him Reggie! We were silly boys in those days!

As I drove up the mountain to your gravesite today, I reflected upon you asking me to see if Mrs. Opal Duke would sell a little piece of her land adjacent to the Lewis Back Cemetery. I gladly did so and to my delight she consented. We went up on the hill and measured off the lot. You purchased it and when sister Deanna passed through the turbid veil, you named the cemetery, Deanna Back Addition. You could not have picked a lovelier spot high on that mountain. You saw to it that the area was cleared, and a nice chain link fence was placed around it. For some reason, my small service offered me comfort, as I looked at where you would be laid to rest. I brought a small flag that I had placed at the waterfall (yes, the place we all used to play) and placed it at the head of your gravesite. I waited for the procession but something within me said I was unworthy to be there when you came home to join those that had gone before, so I left. But not without leaving tears of loss, regret, and forgiveness for not being the man I should have been.

Dear Russ, now you are gone. Link by link your brothers and sisters were taken. Deanna, Janet, David and now, you. Arlin is the only one of the siblings left. He is like me, an adult orphan. But there is no doubt that he will carry the Blair/Whitaker name forward with the same tenacity and dignity he has always done. You can rest assured that he will remember and share those times with others. Your Aunt Berma will carry one your legacy and speak of you often, as will your wife, Connie, and son Chris. Rest assured they are your voice.

Finally, know that my love for you will never diminish and my admiration of you will not fade. Though our days of childhood innocence have gone there is no doubt in this fielder's heart that you were one of the best of us. Now, you earned your rest upon that mountain. Better yet, you have earned your place among the angels through accepting the unconditional love of Jesus Christ. Best of all we will see each other again after the rest, the resurrection, and the reunion. So you see, we Will live forever…

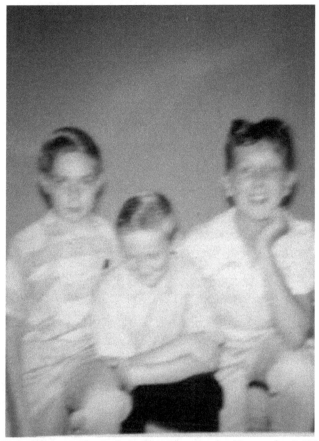

(Me, Russell and Arlin James in Detroit, MI)

"Though the heart cries for what it lost, the soul smiles for what it has found."

*"Let the little children come to me, and do not hinder them, for **the** kingdom **of** God belongs to such as these.* Luke 18:16

DOING UNTO OTHERS

"Do Unto as you would have them do unto you."
Luke 6:31

*"Do not let any unwholesome talk come out of
your mouths, but only what is helpful for building
others up according to their needs, that it may
benefit those who listen. And do not grieve the
Holy Spirit of God, with whom you were sealed for
the day of redemption. Get rid of all bitterness,
rage and anger, brawling and slander, along **with**
every form of malice. Be kind and compassionate
to one another, forgiving each other, just as in
Christ God forgave you."*
Ephesians 4:29-32

Sometimes you can just be still and see how the 'real world' has changed. I had one of those moment today. I wish to share it with you, but not in a condescending judgmental way. I rather take this as a lesson for all of us to better understand the power of a smile and influence.

I had occasion to visit a dear friend of mine that happens to be the CEO of a rather large organization. I went in and spoke to the receptionist who was sorting through a large pile of mail. She didn't look up. I said I wanted to speak to my friend. Without looking up, she asked me did I have an appointment. I said no but it would only take a moment. She looked at me and must not have been impressed. I wouldn't have been either, as I was in blue jeans and an untucked shirt. I even had my old shoes on my feet!

She asked me my name and I gave it to her. She called and informed the CEO I was there. He acknowledged me and told her that he would see me in a moment. I took a seat in the lobby and thought I would just observe for a while. After all, that trait comes from years of serving as a behavioral specialist for the state of Kentucky.

In a couple of minutes, a young lady comes out of the office, walks within five feet of me, turns to the receptionist and without glancing my way, began talking about lunch. She went back into her office and I smiled to myself. A few minutes later, some of the office staff started signing out for lunch. I counted eight that passes by me. I noted that none looked in my direction, didn't smile and seemed to be focused on the world of cellular phones. I couldn't help but overhear a couple of comments. Let us just say they were 'unwholesome' and leave it at that.

Frankly, I was amazed as the manner in which they all seemed so 'lifeless'. I witnessed no joy, no connection to anyone other than their own personal world and certainly not to a person waiting in the lobby. Everyone seemed to be caught up in their own little world. I wondered if their boss knew.

A few more minutes passed before my old friend came to the door. I stood up and he not only shook my hand but gave me one of those old college bear hugs! I could see that the receptionist was surprised to see the reception I received! Usually, he would call the receptionist and have the visitor walk back to his office.

We went back into his office and began talking. Of course, the conversation soon turned to the good old days, the grade school, high school, and college days. We laughed and for a few minutes we were young again.

We began talking about the modern world and how everyone was so involved with themselves that they forget people around them. What a perfect moment for me to gently mentioned what I observed. As I shared my experience, I could tell by the continence of his facial features he wasn't a happy camper! He listened and after I shared what I saw, he reminded me of all the times I was at his house and how we had to say 'yes mam' or 'yes sir' at the beginning and ending of our conversation with an elder. We shared tales of olden days when manners reigned supreme and 'thank you, excuse me and your welcome' were mandated terms. He said he had pride in his company showing and making a person feel welcome or uncomfortable. He looked at me and then said, "Let's take a walk."

As we walked down the corridor, we encountered so many smiling faces! He introduced me to several of his administrative staff. Everyone I met seemed so friendly and greeted me like a long-lost friend. After a tour, we went to the receptionist area. He introduced me, and I have to say that lady acted like I was the cat's meow! She was jumping through all the social hoops. I had to laugh within my spirit!

While I was talking to her, he looked at the list of those who had signed out while I was waiting. He asked the receptionist to call them to the conference room and for her to join us. To be honest, I was getting a little nervous because I recalled his demeanor when he used to get upset during those good old college years.

We went into the conference room and for a few lingering seconds, he didn't say a word. Then he spoke a one-word sentence. The word was respect. I thought it was quite appropriate considering that Mrs. Aretha Franklin had made it a national theme that still is carried forward today. He got a felt tip marker and wrote the following on the board: Character is something you do when no one is watching. He looked at those in the conference room, then looked at me and smiled.

"Butch, let's go have lunch." I smiled at the those present, thanked them for their assistance and left with my old friend. I do believe the message was received loud and clear to that secretarial pool.

Friends isn't it funny how perceived power can change the mood and direction of others. If I had went in wearing a suit and tie, all the while carrying an empty briefcase, there is no doubt I would have received a different welcome. I'll bet you a dollar to a donut I would have been given the courtesy that would be perceived by my clothes. In my youth I recall a short story about a man who wore different uniforms and people treated him as they perceived his role to be. The story was called, Clothes Make the Man.

"Show yourself in all respects to be a model of good works, and in your teaching show integrity, dignity and sound speech that cannot be condemned so that an opponent may be put to shame, having nothing evil to say about you."
Titus 2:7-8

FRIENDS

*"A man who has friends must himself be friendly,
But there is a friend who sticks closer than a
brother."*
Proverbs 18:24

As I reflect upon my life, I must acknowledge the role that friends have played. I am not talking about acquaintances, but rather friends that have become family. There are those unreliable friends. There are those who profess to be friends, but when you need them, they are no where to be found. Many friends do not necessarily mean they will come to your aid. So, I ask what is a friend? This is my definition.

A friend is someone who offers genuine love and friendship. He or she can be counted on when the going gets rough and stand by your side. A friend is honest and will gently (and sometimes sternly) correct you while offering their support. A friend is steadfast and can be counted on in your life. Trustworthiness is one of the virtues of friendship. A friend speaks truthfully and when his/her word is given, you can take it to the bank!

When I think of friendship, the relationship between Jonathan and David comes to mind. Jonathan stood between David and King Saul at the risk of his own life. Upon Jonathan's death,

David openly wept and lamented his death. (II
Samuel 1:25-26. I also recall the love that John
had for Christ, as well as the love he had for John.
In fact, Jesus was and IS a friend to all sinners.
(Luke 7:34)

I can think of so many that have befriended me
over the years. I also can think of all those
enemies I have made that should have been
friends. Friend it is never too late to make up for
those mistakes. God's love for us compels us to
love our enemies. He set the standard and gave His
Son as an example for us to follow when it comes
to friendship.

The greatest example is Jesus Christ. I think of
His love for Lazarus. The Bible tells us that he
cried when he heard of Lazarus death (John
11:35). I believe Christ loved him and hearing the
mournful cries of Martha and Mary stirred His
compassion and empathy. I also believe His tears
were for All who were lost. Jesus compassion was
proved at the cross! For He is the resurrection and
the life; he who believe in Him will live even if he
dies! (John 11:25)

Are you a friend that sticks closer than a brother?
If not, join the many who have failed in the past as
friends. But the good news is that we CAN be a
true friend if we follow the example of our Lord
and Savior. We CAN prove to be trustworthy,

loving, caring and honest with our brothers/sisters that we all friends. God gave us so many examples in His love letters to us. And did He not promise us that He would never forsake us or leave us?! We are more than conquerors when we are under the wings of our Heavenly Fathers. He is our best friend and though I am so unworthy to say this, He has chosen me and has become my 'bestest' friend.

"As the Father has loved me, so have I loved you. Now remain in my love. If you keep my commands, you will remain in my love, just as I have kept my Father's commands and remain in his love. I have told you this so that my joy may be in you and that your joy may be complete. My command is this: Love each other as I have loved you. Greater love has no one than this: to lay down one's life for one's friends. You are my friends if you do what I command. I no longer call you servants, because a servant does not know his master's business. Instead, I have called you friends, for everything that I learned from my Father I have made known to you. You did not choose me, but I chose you and appointed you so that you might go and bear fruit—fruit that will last—and so that whatever you ask in my name the Father will give you. This is my command: Love each other." John 15:9-17

VISIONS AND DREAMS

"Where there is no revelation, people cast off restraint; but blessed is the one who heeds wisdom's instruction"
Proverbs 29:18

I do not wish to be a braggard or a vain person. In fact, I was reluctant to write this, but found myself revisiting the following in my thoughts. So, I decided to put my thoughts to the pen and hopefully the point I wish to make will be realized by others. Please keep in mind that this is NOT about me, but rather it is about God and the manner in which he inspires us all to do His bidding. He is the master architect and we are merely His workers. To God goes all the glory and praises for His vision for His children.

Some people say that I have been blessed with a passion to do things in my life to pay homage to others and to remember my ancestors' services and sacrifices. It has nothing to do with ego but rather it is all about Him. Some might call it a vision, but I think of it as a calling of sorts. I know I am different, and I am thankful for that, as I believe each person walks his/her own path. That is what is wonderful about God's plan in our lives. He gives us free will to make choices. He guides us and shelters us with his love but all of us have had our share of sadness, tears, loss, and trials. That, my friends, is when He surrounds us with His love. All we need do is remember a poem written by Mary Stevenson in 1936. It is called:

Footprints in the Sand

One night I dreamed I was walking along the beach with the Lord. Many scenes from my life flashed across the sky.

In each scene I noticed footprints in the sand. Sometimes there were two sets of footprints, other times there was one only.

This bothered me because I noticed that during the low periods of my life, when I was suffering from anguish, sorrow, or defeat, I could see only one set of footprints, so I said to the Lord,

"You promised me Lord, that if I followed you, you would walk with me always. But I have noticed that during the most trying periods of my life there has only been one set of footprints in the sand. Why, when I needed you most, have you not been there for me?"

The Lord replied, "The years when you have seen only one set of footprints, my child, is when I carried you."

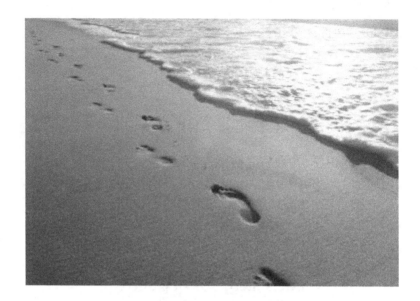

I have found that when he cradles me in His arms, I most content. I have found such peace, such joy, such love to move my soul. I have found during those precious moments I am most inspired. One of the ways I feel inspired is to work on monuments honoring our God, Country, and Veterans.

Over the years I have been privy to work on several projects. Some of them were large, but most small to the common eye. Yet, the monuments are a testament to our Christian way of life and to those willing to offer all for our very freedoms. Below are some of the markers, monuments I have been privileged to partake in having them come alive.

--Westwood Cemetery Project-We not only set over 30 markers, we also generated money to have a 6x3 marker placed at the abandoned portion of the cemetery, researched several of those lost souls resting place, and left 2 markers with a poem I had written along with a saying (I asked God) beside a bench we purchased.

--WE have set hundreds of markers honoring our Union/Confederate soldiers not only in Letcher County but the region and tri-states. We even set one in 96, South Carolina.

--We set and had a wondrous dedication honoring the abandoned graves of Black Coal Miners of Carbon Glow. I remember Arthur Christian singing, Bernard Watts speaking, the military salute by the Sons of Confederate Veterans, and we had over 180 people to attend. I was selected to be the master of ceremonies.

--Monuments honoring Coal Miners at Hemphill (names of those miners were from the research by my class), dedication and continued efforts to honor ALL miners killed while making a living for their families.

--Participated in hundreds of dedications from Revolutionary, Civil War, World War II & II, Korea, Vietnam, to current day. We dedicated the graves of Native Americans, such as Greenberry Thomas, Golden Hawk Sizemore and others.

--911 project (designed and developed by Alternative Education and Day Treatment students)

--Ira Mullins Monument on Pound Gap and the Coal Miners marker

--The desecrated gravesite on Perkins Branch (it is being cut as we speak)

--THEN there were many projects outside of KY, such as the KY Monument in Vicksburg, Succession Hill in Abbeville and so forth.

My point is that all these projects started out as visions and dreams. This we know: Prayer changes things. Add a passion and desire to develop a project, well my friends, all things are possible!

The Bible teaches us that "Where there is no vision, the people perish". It is my firm belief that all of us possess a vision, a dream, a what if, but sometimes it takes motivation, determination, and sacrifice to see that vision and that dream to materialize. Does not the Bible tell us that God created? Does the Bible not say that we were created in His image? Did not Jesus say to go out and be fishers of men? Through vision, through leadership, through commitment and sacrifice, we can realize our destiny.

I am but one voice. I am but one man. I have done nothing to have my laurels sung. The reason is very simple. I am nothing more than a clay pot being filled by my Creator. I am the pen in the Master's hand. I deserve NO glory, but He deserves all glory! He is the one who plants the seeds and we are merely the farmers. The care takers and the keepers of the keys.

Friends, what are your visions and dreams? Do they serve the glory of God and your fellow human beings? Are they worthy enough to be blessed by Him and guided by His hands? We, His people, must remember and reflect upon our vision and dreams so the rising generation will have a path to follow.

"Remove not the ancient landmark which thy fathers have set."
Proverbs 22:28

BOB

"But if anyone does not provide for his relatives, and especially for members of his household, he has denied the faith and is worse than an unbeliever."
I Timothy 5:8

Bob was a busy man. He was a man of influence and was respected by his peers for his innovative ideas and the manner in which he could get things done. His work was his life. He was a go getter! That is, everywhere but home. For he had forgotten that everything important is invisible to the eye.

He seemed never to have time for his ailing mother. He even resented her for trying to get him to slow down and 'smell the roses'. She was always wanting to talk, and he just didn't have the time. Someday we can talk but not now he'd say.

It was the same with his wife. She wanted family time, but he had business on his mind and always planning for the next day at work. The strain of a one-sided relationship soon wore her down and before long, she left with the kids. He justified her leaving by saying to himself that it was best and besides, he could support the kids better with the extra time he would have working. Besides, once all the work gets done, he'd make it up to them and they would do things differently.

Each day he found himself surrounded by people that were coworkers and colleagues. Yet, in reality, none were really friends. He chose work over friends and family. Besides, there would be time later when he could visit with his friends and make new ones.

One day while in a conference, his boss received a telephone call. He answered and listened to the person talking. Slowly, he hung up and turning to Bob, he asked him to step outside. Bob was perplexed because he was right in the middle of his presentation that he worked hours to prepare. What could be more important than what he was doing to be dragged away. Didn't his boss realize this was something that had to be done now. There was no time to talk in private, but he was the boss.

Bob's boss took him into an office and sighed.

"Bob, I don't know how to tell you this," his voice shaken with emotion.

"Go ahead and say it so I can get back to my presentation," Bob replied.

"Bob, there's been an accident. Your wife and children are gone," he stated with his head bowed.

"What do you mean gone?" Bob asked.

"Son, they are dead," He softly replied.

"No, they can't be. I was going to visit them this weekend after I get the work done," Bob said in total denial of the news.

"You need to go home Bob," his boss stated.

"If there is anything I can do, let me know," with a pat on Bob's shoulder, his boss went back into the meeting.

Bob was stunned. There were so many things he had planned to do once he got caught up and earned the promotion, along with the bonus. He was going to take the kids to Disney World and his wife on a cruise. He was going to make up for all the times he put work above family. He was...

As he drove home, a chilling realization overtook him, and he could not comprehend his feelings. They flooded his soul with sorrow. Why didn't he do the things with them instead of putting them off. Why didn't he show love and spend time, precious time with them? Oh, how he cried over the things he didn't do. He cried out to God to give back his family and that precious time he squandered. There was a silence in the heavens.

All of his tomorrows came crashing down on him that day.

Friends, how many of us are like Bob? Friends, there are times in our lives that we don't see the trees for the forest. There are times when we find ourselves so busy with things that we forget about living. Bob learned through a terrible tragedy that all is essential is truly invisible to the eye. Love, family, joy, peace, and friends make up life and work just makes a living.

Years ago, I had the privilege of teaching a college class called, Human Potential. One of the books I used was Living, Loving and Learning. Leo Buscaglia was the author and he had so many words of wisdom, poems to inspire and truths to touch the heart. One of the poems I loved was called, Things you didn't do. I share it in hopes that it stirs your spirit and helps you realize what is truly important.

"Things You Didn't Do"
Author Unknown

Remember the day I borrowed your brand new car
and I dented it?
I thought you'd kill me, but you didn't.
And remember the time I dragged you to the
beach, and you said it would rain, and it did?
I thought you'd say, "I told you so." But you didn't.

Do you remember the time I flirted will all the
guys to make you jealous, and you were?
I thought you'd leave me, but you didn't.
Do you remember the time I spilled strawberry pie
all over your car rug?
I thought you'd hit me, but you didn't.
And remember the time I forgot to tell you the
dance was formal and you showed up in jeans?
I thought you'd drop me, but you didn't.
Yes, there were lots of things you didn't do.
But you put up with me, and you loved me, and
you protected me.
There were lots of things I wanted to make up to
you when you returned from Viet Nam.
But you didn't.

Friends, are you worried? Are you making a living
instead of making a life? Are you tending to the
duties of man instead of the commandments for the
glory to God? Relax and breath! Friends, time is
slipping away and no one knows the appointed
hour of another's passing. But take heart, it is not
to late! You can turn this very moment and follow
those things that are essential to living a good life.

If you recall the thieves on the cross dying beside
of Jesus. On laughed and made fun but the other
begged Christ to remember him. Recall His words
to the thief. *"Verily I say unto thee, today shalt
thou be with me in paradise."* Luke 23:43.
Friends, don't allow this world to take from you

what God has promised you. He has said you would have joy in great abundance. The answer is to follow Christ as His disciple, lean not unto your own understanding, and love above all things. The simple steps of salvation takes away the complexity of the modern world.

"Now as they went on their way, Jesus entered a village. And a woman named Martha welcomed him into her house. And she had a sister called Mary, who sat at the Lord's feet and listened to his teaching. But Martha was distracted with much serving. And she went up to him and said, "Lord, do you not care that my sister has left me to serve alone? Tell her then to help me." But the Lord answered her, "Martha, Martha, you are anxious and troubled about many things, but one thing is necessary. Mary has chosen the good portion, which will not be taken away from her."
Luke 10:38-42

THE SNAKE AND THE SAW

"A soft answer turneth away wrath: but grievous words stir up anger."
Proverbs 15:1

There are so many stories I heard while sitting on the front porch of my uncles' house. The ones that are most vivid are those of snakes. Uncle Charlie would talk of the time when he was in Africa and sat on what he thought was a log. When the log started moving, he realized it was a giant snake. Then Uncle Arlie would talk about copper heads mating for life and if you killed one, its mate would come looking for you.

I must admit that I wouldn't walk to the outhouse after dark no matter how bad I had to 'go'! There was one story that lingers in my mind and I am not sure if I can get it right, but it has a lesson. I call it the snake and the saw.

Uncle Charlie was a carpenter and had a bunch of tools he kept in a tin shed he had made. One morning he went out to get his tools and place them on the tool belt. There lying tightly coiled around his saw was a dead snake. He said he couldn't figure out what happened until he started thinking.

The snake must have crawled into the shed looking for a mouse. The snake must have crawled over a hand saw and was cut by the sharp blades (Uncle Charlie use to keep his tools in top condition and his saw was always sharper than a razor). The snake must have thought something attacked it, so it turned a bit at the saw. Of course, this made its mouth bleed. Then the snake wrapped himself around his adversary and tightened its coils. That led to even more cuts and blood. The snake must have thought he was in a battle for his life and became angry. The snake's tightened and coiled around the saw in a death grip but the harder it squeezed, the more it bled. Finally, its anger and stubbornness led to its death.

I have pondered that story for over fifty years and finally come to realize the significance of my Uncle's lesson. Sometimes in life we, allow our stubbornness (or as my mother used to say-being set in our ways) and anger destroy us when we can simply let them go. I know letting go of that 'saw' is easier said than done, but when situations are beyond your control, the only answer is in letting go.

The Bible speaks of anger and stubbornness. One of my favorite verses can be found in Ephesians 4:26-31. *"In your anger do not sin: Do not let the sun go down while you are still angry, and do not give the devil a foothold. Anyone who has been stealing must steal no longer, but must work, doing something useful with their own hands, that they may have something to share with those in need. Do not let any unwholesome talk come out of your mouths, but only what is helpful for building others up according to their needs, that it may benefit those who listen. And do not grieve the Holy Spirit of God, with whom you were sealed for the day of redemption. Get rid of all bitterness, rage and anger, brawling and slander, along with every form of malice."*

TENACITY OF SPIRIT

*"O death, where is thy sting? O grave, where is
thy victory?"*
I Corinthians 15:55

For some reason that word is special to me. I
guess because I have seen some friends with a
tenacity of spirit. They still remain in my mind as
heroes.

The definition of tenacity is the quality or fact to
be able to grip something firmly. Another
dictionary definition of tenacity is to be very
determined. To me that means persistence.

I remember when I first found out about her
cancer. She was my dear friend and a dear friend
in her own right. She was having headaches and
went for a routine checkup. The MRI revealed a
large tumor and the diagnosis was that she had
brain cancer. The doctor told her she had six
months to a year to live.

I recall when she came home. I was invited to
have supper with the family unaware of their
plight. Her husband met me at the door and asked
me to take a walk with him. While walking he told
me the grim news. I didn't know what to say or
what to do.

We went back into the house and there she was cooking away. She greeted me with that warm smile and said dinner would be ready in a few minutes. I thought to myself, how could she be so uplifted and cooking for me and her family. We sat down and ate. The conversation was casual as usual, but I kept glancing at her. On occasion she caught me looking, and I looked away and tried to not draw attention to my nervous mannerisms.

After we finished supper, I always helped clean off the table and carrying dishes to the kitchen. I can still see her putting the scraps in the wastebasket. I didn't know what to say and when I talked to her, she could tell I was nervous. She smiled and said something I will always remember. She said, "Don't worry, this isn't anything God can't handle. I plan to outlive the doctor!"

I looked into her eyes and saw it. Within her being was such a wondrous Tenacity of spirit! She kept her word. She lived sixteen years after the diagnose and did outlive her doctor.

What amazed me most was her upbeat manner. No matter how bad she felt, she would always say that she felt great. She was determined. She had tenacity and a positive attitude that she would live until she died. Her tenacity of spirit has inspired others that are terminally ill.

I had another dear friend who was diagnosed with brain cancer. The tumor was large and the surgery long. Upon awakening, the first thing out of her mouth was that she wanted a Big Mac! Now that is tenacity of spirit and I love that person as if she was my own offspring.

The Bible tells us that no one knows the appointed time of our passing. Don't believe me? Read God's word in Matthew 24:26. "But of that day and hour no one knows, not even the angels of heaven, but My Father only."

There is victory in Jesus, our precious redeemer! He is the resurrection and the life. He will never forsake you or abandon you. If you believe and accept Him as your one and only Savior, you only rest before the resurrection and then the reunion of His saints.

"Brothers, we do not want you to be ignorant about those who fall asleep, or to grieve like the rest of men, who have no hope. We believe that Jesus died and rose again and so we believe that God will bring with Jesus those who have fallen asleep in him."
I Thessalonians 4:13-14

I ASKED GOD

"And whatsoever ye shall ask in my name, that I will do, that the Father may be glorified in the Son." John 14:13

I wish to offer something I found years ago while reenacting. This wondrous testament of faith was found during the War Between the States on a dead soldier. It is an affirmation and to me, it symbolizes the answering of prayer. May all your prayers be answered.

I asked God for strength, that I might achieve.
I was made weak, that I might learn humbly to obey.
I asked for health, that I might do greater things.
I was given infirmity, that I might do better things.
I asked for riches that I might be happy.
I was given poverty, that I might be wise.
I asked for power that I might have the praise of men.
I was given weakness, that I might feel the need of God.
I asked for all things, that I might enjoy life.
I was given life, that I might enjoy all things.
I got nothing that I asked for but got everything I had hoped for.
Almost despite myself, my unspoken prayers were answered.
I am, among all people, most richly blessed.

CPSIA information can be obtained
at www.ICGtesting.com
Printed in the USA
BVHW041303110821
614201BV00013B/309

9 781983 818486